WOMEN AND ORDERS

WOMEN
AND ORDERS

Edited by
Robert J. Heyer

PAULIST PRESS
New York/Paramus/Toronto

Library of Congress
Catalog Card Number: 74-80262

ISBN: 0-8091-1841-6

Published by Paulist Press
Editorial Office: 1865 Broadway, N.Y., N.Y. 10023
Business Office: 400 Sette Drive, Paramus, N.J. 07652

Printed and bound in the
United States of America

Contents

Foreword

The question of the ordination of women to the priesthood has moved to the forefront of theological controversy in recent years, prompting a rash of books and magazine essays. The issue stems not only from the renewed interest of the Catholic Church in the nature of its priesthood, but also, and perhaps primarily, from the efforts of women to achieve and a new and deeper understanding of their nature and its potential and of the various myths that have relegated them to a subsidiary position in the human race.

One of the most critical theaters for this development of feminine consciousness lies within the realm of religion. Betty Friedan, whose book *The Feminine Mystique* sparked the women's liberation movement, recently explained that this struggle necessitates a confrontation with the organized churches because these are so largely responsible for the poor self-image of their female members. Women are burdened not only by overt discrimination by men but also by a profound attitudinal discrimination in themselves. And the denial of the priesthood to women exemplifies the whole gamut of theological and cultural myths taught to women by their pastors to justify a second-class, auxiliary status in the Church.

What are the theological and sociological consequences of the dictum of the Catholic Church which limits the ordained priesthood to males, and celibate males at that? Seven authors confront the most vital component of the question in these pages.

Rosemary Radford Ruether leads off by stating flatly that the notion that only a male can represent Christ is theologically suspect. It was Jesus' human nature, not his male sexuality that the early Fathers were at pains to defend. To make maleness essential to the incarnation would in traditional orthodoxy have excluded women not only from ordination but also from salvation. As the theologians maintained, "that which is not assumed (by the human nature of Christ) is not saved." Mrs. Ruether argues that the psychological root of the cleric's antipathy to women in the ministry stems from the dualism which places male/spirit/transcendence over against female body/creature. What is good is male; what is evil is female!

Ruth Tiffany Barnhouse, a psychiatrist and an Episcopalian, looks at the ordination of women in terms of the symbolism of the Eucharist. The greatest opposition to women priests, she notes, exists in those churches which place the greatest stress on the ritual mystery of the Eucharist. Yet the bread and wine offered in the sacrifice represent humanity which includes both men and women. Every man and woman has some of the traits considered characteristic of the other sex, Dr. Barnhouse observes. Admitting women to full partnership in the priesthood would permit a union of the masculine and feminine principles.

Emily C. Hewitt, an ordained deacon in the Episcopal Church, believes the all-male priesthood is undergirded by the notion that equates maleness with creativity, with the priest offering the Mass exercising creative powers similar to those of God. She points out that Israel repudiated the idea of sexuality in God: Yahweh is neither he nor she; as creator and Lord, he embraces and transcends both sexes. She also argues that the sex, race and ancestry of Jesus and his twelve apostles were intended to fulfill the messianic prophecy under the old covenant, not to determine the nature of ministry in the Church of the new covenant.

Gregory Baum points out that our present hierarchical priesthood was not original. Theologians now believe that the gradual historical development that led to the monarchial episcopate was tested by the evangelical norms of Christian leadership and accepted by the Christian community as due to the guidance of the Holy Spirit. But, the Canadian theologian says, the theologians are bound to hold, on the selfsame principle, that this development could continue. There is need to test whether the present hierarchical ministry is too closely tied with an oppressive and worldly structure of authority and whether the priesthood has, in fact, become a caste. Since people are becoming aware of the extent of the oppression of women down through the ages, Father Baum suggests that the Church ought to reveal through its ordained leadership that men and women are destined to be equal.

Ann Kelley and Anne Walsh, Catholic university chaplains, oppose the ordination of women precisely because the priesthood is a power caste and an entry into a power structure that opens the way to privilege. They say that ordination is a questionable goal for women because it will interfere with their traditional ministry of service and also that this office is not necessary for ministry.

Thomas F. O'Meara, O.P., takes the opposite route by suggesting that the Church should diversify its criteria for ordination and should ordain members of the Christian community for many forms of service, including those which women have been performing for centuries but without any public commissioning or status. Ministry, the Dominican theologian observes, is not identical with lifestyle, and ordination should not be limited to celibate males.

Clara Marie Henning, a canonist, argues for both a married priesthood and women priests because, she explains, the sections of canon law which wall off priests from almost all contacts with women in the effort to preserve mandatory celibacy create a mentality which makes it impossible for clerics to see any positive value in such ordination.

The question is: Should women be ordained as ministers in the Church? This immediately implies many questions. What have been the results of many centuries of male priesthood? What is authentic ministry in the Church? What is the Spirit revealing in our day for the needs of the Church? Reflective reading of these pages will certainly stimulate your thinking and praying concerning women's ordination.

Male Clericalism
and the Dread of Women

Rosemary Radford Ruether

THE arguments which have been given recently
by the Roman Catholic hierarchy against the ordination of women, i.e., the maleness of Jesus and
the apostles, are surprising. They are weak theologically and have little background in traditional thinking. The standard quip that "Jesus also only appointed Jews as apostles" points to the untenability
of assuming the sociological accidents of the primitive apostolate as eternal norms for the ministry of
the Church. As Emily Hewitt has pointed out, Jewishness was as much a requirement as maleness for
the New Testament concept of Jesus and the Twelve.
Jesus, as the representative of Israel, and the Twelve,
as the representatives of the Twelve tribes, must be
both Jewish and male, for the Jewish congregation
counted only males as members of the congregation.
These norms have been abandoned by the Church.
The maleness of Jesus and the apostles is just as
sociologically contingent to that setting as is the
requirement that they be Jews.

The argument that Jesus was male and, therefore, that only a male can represent Christ, is theologically suspect. In any case, it is doubtful that one
should regard the priest as "incarnating" Jesus in
any such literal sense. The traditional understanding
of the incarnation never meant, as its center, the incarnation of Jesus in the male sex. Rather the point
was the incarnation in "human nature." Traditional
Calcedonian orthodoxy even denied to Jesus a
"human person," making his person that of the divine Logos! (Is the person of God sexually male?)
We might want to alter this kind of orthodoxy from
other points of view, but it is clear that it understood
the essential character of the incarnation, not in
terms of Jesus' male sexuality, but in terms of generic "human nature." Indeed to make maleness essential to the incarnation would have, in traditional
orthodoxy, excluded women, not merely from ordination, but from salvation! In fact all of the theological arguments against the ordination of women are
based on views which, taken literally, would also
exclude women from baptism. All define women in
terms which exclude them from full humanity and
capacity for grace. As the ancient Patristic theologians put it, "that which is not assumed (by the
human nature of Christ) is not saved." Hence the
human nature of Christ cannot be defined in terms
which make maleness essential, but in terms of that
generic human nature which, in Genesis, is "both
male and female." Anything less than this would
define the essential work of the incarnation in a way
that would exclude women from the fruits of the incarnation, i.e., redemption.

However, even when these arguments are refuted theologically and shown to be sociologically contingent, we have, I believe, only begun to sound the real depths of the resistance to the ordination of women by a male hierarchy. We know now that women did serve in various leadership capacities in the apostolic Church. Moreover one of the striking characteristics of Jesus is his unconventionality toward women. According to Jewish Law, one was never to look at or talk to a woman who was not one's wife; a rule Jesus broke to the astonishment of the disciples. To be touched by a woman with a flow of blood was to suffer instant contamination; an idea Jesus also rejects. Women also were forbidden to study Torah, so Jesus, in praising Mary over Martha, was reversing female role stereotypes. When Paul, in his letters, is attempting to reassert the male leadership principles of the synagogue, he does so against what has become the practice of female participation in his own churches. Moreover he does so, not on the grounds of the maleness of Jesus or the apostles, but on the grounds of the "orders of Creation." According to this analogy, male overlordship and female passivity symbolize the relation of God to Creation, and hence the relationship of Christ to the Church. Krister Stendahl, in his magisterial *The Bible and the Role of Women*, has fully refuted the tenability of this argument from the orders of Creation as binding on the leadership principles of the Christian community. This analogy is seen as drawn from the current social subjugation of women, and so can have no continuing authority in the order of redemption represented by the Church.

Thomas Aquinas and other medieval thinkers followed an Aristotelian version of this same argument which equated the social subjugation of women with a subordination intrinsic to the "order of Creation." According to Aristotle, women (also slaves and non-Greeks) represented the naturally servile personality, *vis-à-vis* the free, Greek male. Social order was analogous to the hierarchical relation of mind over body. The free Greek male represented the dominion of the rational over the carnal or the material principle essential for order and "justice." Aristotle defines women, biologically, as "misbegotten males," who lack full rationality. Aquinas accepted a version of this Aristotelian definition of the nature of women and argued that women (and serfs) could not be ordained because they lack the "eminence" required to incarnate leadership. Lacking full rationality, they cannot represent the divine Logos (Christ). For the same reason their natures are incapable of receiving the "sign" of ordination. This argument, again, if taken literally, would exclude women, not only from ordination, but from normative human nature.

Sexism: The Result of Misappropriated Dualisms

Behind the superficial arguments about the maleness of Jesus and the apostles, then, we must perceive a much deeper misogynism which is the real psychological foundation of the need to exclude women from the ministry. Sexism, or the inferiorization of women, is based, symbolically, on misappropriated dualisms. The basic dialectics of human existence:body/soul; carnality/spirituality; Becoming/

Being; seeming/Truth; death/life: these dualisms are symbolized in terms of female and male and socially projected as the "natures" of men and women. The meaning of the "feminine," then, is modeled, especially in classical ascetic cultures, on the images of the lower self and world. Autonomous spiritual selfhood is imaged (by men, the cultural creators of this view) as intrinsically "male," while the "feminine" becomes the symbol of the repressed, subjugated and dreaded "abysmal side of man."

This sociological projection of the dialectics of existence as "male" and "female" has, as its ultimate expression, the God-nature dualism. In Patriarchal religions God comes to be seen as the "wholly other" outside of and above "nature." The relation of God and nature is imaged in terms of subject-object dualism. God is seen as analogous to consciousness: a transcendent Subject that reduces Creation to the status of an object or "created thing." God is made in the image of the body-alienated "male Ego" over against nature, as the sphere to be dominated and subjugated. The relationship of God and Creation is patterned after the language of patriarchal conjugality. God is the "sky-Husband/Father" over against the earth as "wife." In the Bible this analogy is transferred to the relation of Yahweh and Israel and, in Christianity, to the relation of Christ to the Church. The Church is the passive, dependent "Bride" of patriarchal marriage in relation to the divine "Bridegroom."

One must suppose from this that the representatives of the Church ought, therefore, to be female! But, of course, the leadership of the Church sees itself as representing, not the Church before God (i.e.,

Mary), but rather God before the Church! Hence the same imagery of hierarchical patriarchal conjugality, as the relation of Christ to the Church, is introduced to express the relationship of the clergy to the laity. The people are the passive dependent "child-women" before the male Father-husband figure of the clergy, who represent God or Christ. The Church becomes split into a "male" active principle, hierarchically related to a "female" passive principle. The people cease to be seen as having self-generating capacities for leadership which can bless, teach or ordain. Instead they must receive "the Word" from outside and above themselves. The laity assumes the prone position before the representatives of the transcendent Father-God, who brings all grace and truth "from above."

The Church molded its self-imagery in terms which symbolically exclude the possibility of women representing this hierarchical function. Underneath this image of transcendent maleness and creaturely "femininity," we must see older and more unconscious ways in which the female is seen to stand for the dark abysmal "side of man." The notion that women are intrinsically "unclean" and that menstruation and other female bodily functions constitute a dangerous "mana" that would "pollute" the Holy Places, was strong in Judaism. It was taken over in modified form in Christian Canon Law. Menstruation, as a source of uncleanliness, was the chief pretext for suppressing the ancient order of Deaconesses in the Patristic period. Until recent times it was believed to be more "pious" if women did not come to communion when they were menstruating. This view is still inculcated in traditional Catholic and Orthodox women. To this image of woman as "unclean," Catholic spirituality added a heightened perception of women as sexual threat over against a "male" spirituality. Women were seen as representing the "carnal," *vis-à-vis* male intellectuality, spirituality and virtue. The sacred sphere becomes the preserve of this male spirituality, which must be protected from contamination by "female" sexuality. This view of woman as sexual threat is deeply ingrained in the psychology of a celibate priesthood, although the same mentality has by no means vanished from Protestantism, despite its married ministry. As Clara Maria Henning has shown in her article on women in Catholic Canon Law (in my forthcoming book on *Images of Women in the Jewish and Christian Traditions;* Simon and Schuster), most of the references to women in Canon Law have to do with excluding them from contact with priests, both personally and in relation to the sanctuary.

These traditional ways of symbolizing the duality of God/nature and soul/body as male and female received a significant reshaping at the hands of modern Romanticism (itself the heir of medieval Mariology and Courtly Love). Today we are more the heirs of this modern "feminine mystique," which overlaid and hid the older misogynism on which it was based. Traditional asceticism saw women as less moral than men. They were the "carnal" over against "male" spirituality. But in Romanticism women typically come to be seen as more moral and even more spiritual than men, although this does not alter the view of them as less rational! By the same token morality and spirituality are sentimentalized and are seen as deriving from women's "exclusive

relation to the Home." In the 19th century the old
dualism of materiality and spirituality *qua* "femininity" and "masculinity" is partially reversed. The
old schism is also translated into the new alienation
that opens up between the home and industrial work.
At this time productive labor was being drawn out of
the Home into the factory, and women were becoming domesticated in a way that had not existed before (bourgeois women, that is). Over against the
view of the industrial work world as a sphere of
alienation destructive of human values, the Home
becomes a compensatory ideology. The Home comes
to represent the sole sphere of personal morality,
over against alienated, impersonal, "materialistic"
work. Now men come to be seen as more "materialistic" and less moral than women, but also more
"realistic." The world of male work is seen as the
"real world," *vis-à-vis* the romanticized myth of the
Home where woman presides. Much of the anti-sex-
uality of the Victorian form of this myth was under-
cut by the Freudian revolution. But the basic form of
the romantic "feminine mystique" still remains as
the language of the modern ideology of the Home
that supports consumer society and the "ladies mag-
azines."

In the feminine mystique morality is sentimentalized. It is privatized and "feminized." "Christian"
values are seen as intrinsically "feminine." Morality
in this sense exists only in the sphere of private inter-
personalism represented by marriage and the Home.
The real world is the realm of materialistic values
and "no-nonsense" technological rationality. Bishops, industrial leaders, politicians and unionists all
pay lip service to this myth of the "feminine" when

they oppose rights for women on the grounds that the true "femininity" of women and their authentic role as "moral nurturers of the race" depend on their staying out of the "dirty rough and tumble" of the real world and remaining "in the Home." This mystifying rhetoric and the sentiments it evokes continue on, despite the fact that, today, large numbers of women do work. This rhetoric does not exclude women from work in reality. Its chief effect is to create a resistance to women in visible leadership roles or work that carries social esteem. It does nothing to prevent women from being structured into the more rote and servile forms of labor.

However, the adoption of the feminine mystique as the image of "Christian morality," by both Catholicism and Protestantism, and their acquiescence to the modern split between the Home and work, moral man and immoral society, mean that the Church finds itself psychically and socially structured into the "feminine sphere." Clergy are out of place in the "real world." So we see a clergy, the heir of patriarchal and misogynist self-images, now serving primarily in the realm of domesticated passified "morality" which society calls "effeminate." This seems to me to be a part of the present identity crisis of the clergy, and a strong element in the almost paranoid resistance of the clergy to women in the ministry. As heirs of these contemptuous views of the "feminine," barely covered by its idealization, the appearance of a woman in that role would unmask the last shreds of authority, revealing the cleric as a man dressed "in skirts." The place where he serves, the values he embodies, belong to the sphere which society calls "feminine."

Transformation of Ministry

This paranoia seems to me to be the psychological root of the antipathy to women in the ministry, which continues all the more virulently when its arguments have been exploded theologically, historically, scripturally or sociologically. The possibility of women in the ministry touches not merely the question of the personal rights of women. For a woman to be regarded as playing the ministerial role regularly (not just exceptionally, as is still the case in denominations which ordain women), the entire psychodynamics, which images the God/man, soul/body, clergy/laity relations in terms of sexual hierarchicalism, would be threatened. A psychological revolution in the way we relate to God, to leadership, to each other, to "nature" and to the relation of the Church to "the world" would be required. The revolution symbolically represented by the ordination of women is profound. We must understand the antipathy to it as much deeper than the flimsy and usually irrational arguments given by its opponents.

But these reasons for the resistance of the clergy to the ordination of women are also the very reasons why we must regard it as necessary. These dualisms, symbolized by the sexual dualism, incarnate a heritage of self-alienation and the social projection of inferior and auxiliary humanity on to women. Racism, anti-Semitism and the subjugation of lower classes and colonized peoples regularly borrow the same language of misappropriated dualisms. The same images justify our ravaging of nature and the amorality of technology. The Church stands as the cultural guardian of these symbols of domination and subjugation. This role must be recognized as an apostasy to the Church's true mission as representative of the liberated Humanity. Instead the Church becomes the chief representative and the sacralizer of the old order, presiding over and blessing that sanctuary where these schisms continue to be preserved.

The ordination of women cannot mean simply the insertion of a few female persons oddly into the present shape of the clergy. It must require a deeper revolution of consciousness that reshapes the psychodynamics of our self, social and world relationships. Leadership must change from its present paternalistic mode to a dialogue form where it is seen more as the skill to evoke the gifts and creative initiatives of others. The "Word" is no longer to be seen as coming from outside the people, from the raised pulpit that reduces the congregation to passive "womenchildren." Rather it springs into being in the midst of the people through dialogue. The Church can begin to become community, rather than an alienation of "male" clerical activity and "female" lay acquiescence. As community, the whole Church is to teach one another, support one another, forgive one another, engage in theological self-reflection on its own ministry to each other. But this overcoming of the language of self-alienation in the Church's internal life must also explode the present encapsulation of the Church in the sphere of privatized sentimentalized "morality." If both the clergy and women have suffered from the encapsulation in the domestic sphere, then they must see each other as allies in a common struggle to overthrow the false schism between "private morality" and the "real world." In order to pray Jesus' prayer that "God's will be done on earth," we must break apart the false schizophrenia between private "feminine" morality and the public world of technological rationality which renders the message of the Church "effete," while the Masters of War go about their "manly" activities. The message of the Church must be seen as the social mandate of human history, rather than private individual "salvation."

Only when men and women are peers in the Church can we create human relationships that express authentic communication and exorcize the evil spirits of injustice and dehumanization that turn women and all oppressed people into fantasized symbols of the negative self. When the mentality of patriarchal hierarchicalism is exorcized from the ministry, then the Church can begin to assume the shape of community representing redemptive reconciliation with God and with each other. Only then can the Church be credible as the sacrament of redeemed humanity, lifting up the redemptive direction of society. Our anthropology must cease to be modeled after sexist doctrines of male hierarchicalism and polar complementarity and become centered in the full human personhood of every individual. For each of us unites all those dualities of thinking and feeling, activity and receptivity, falsely polarized as "masculine" and "feminine." We can begin to relate to each other out of all sides of our being in truly reciprocal ways.

I suspect that the ordination of women must also reshape our image of God. Instead of making God in the image of male superordinate Ego over against subjugated nature, perhaps we should rather think of God as Ground of Being, that divine Matrix of ever reborn creation, out of which all living things both come to be and are renewed. Such a redeeming God cannot be set over against nature, for the same divine Spirit is the ground of both redemption and Creation. The liberation of women from negative projections must also reshape our ways of relating to the bodily and earthly side of existence. The project of human life must cease to be seen as one of domination of nature and subjugation of the bodily self. Rather we must find a language of authentic cooperation; of ecological responsiveness of consciousness to the great web of life, within which we too live and move and have our being. Only then can we redeem our Sister, the Earth, from her bondage of destruction, restoring her as our partner in the creation of that new world where all things can be "very good."

An Examination of the Ordination of Women to the Priesthood in Terms of the Symbolism of the Eucharist

Ruth Tiffany Barnhouse, M.D.

WHEN I began the research for this paper nearly a year ago, I expected that careful study of the psychological symbolism of the sacraments would reveal some hidden but powerful reason why women should not be ordained to the Anglican and Roman priesthoods. I thought this because I knew a number of dedicated feminist women, including myself, who, in spite of being unable to muster any rational argument against it, nevertheless found in themselves a profound disquiet when confronted with the prospect. This seemed quite inexplicable, since none of us had ever experienced any comparable reluctance to enter, or encourage one another to enter, any other profession however traditionally male it might be. To my great surprise, and transitory consternation, I found no hidden symbolic prohibitions against the priesthood of women. On the contrary, I believe I have found some compelling psychological reasons *for* it which in my opinion are equally compelling theologically, and which I will set forth presently.

But first, I should like to offer an explanation for my initial suspicion, since it bears on some of the larger psychological issues. It is perhaps unfashionable in this era of almost chaotically rapid change and intense questioning of received values, to call attention to the role of the Church as the agent of continuity and the defender of tradition. Nevertheless, a society which has no institutions serving this function is in serious danger of collapse. Religion, concerned as it is with the eternal category,[1] is an ideal vehicle for this important role. The consciousness of humankind is clearly involved in the evolutionary process which characterizes the entire universe. But there could be no evolution of consciousness as we know it now without historicity,[2] and no historicity without a background of tradition. It is against this background of relatively stable tradition that we are able to measure and evaluate the constant flux of events so that some intelligent choice can be made about what should be retained, and what discarded. The celebration of religious rituals, involving as it does the archetypal level of our psychological functioning, can perdure almost intact through centuries, even millennia, during which nearly every other outlook and attitude undergoes radical change. For the purpose which I am describing, the rational and intellectual level of meaning of the rites is unimportant. In fact, it can be argued that in all eras, this level of meaning is perhaps of interest mainly to theologians. Theologians themselves are usually aware that the deepest significance of ritual is fundamentally elusive and does not yield to intellectual endeavor. I quote from Father Joseph Kramp, who in 1926 wrote as follows:

> To one who lives with the sacred liturgy, it tells a thousand things which the stranger does not learn. Like a bride, the liturgy reveals her deepest secret only to her beloved. But even to him she does not confide it at once in all its clarity and depth. The privilege of constantly discovering new excellences awakens the happy consciousness that the deepest depths have not been sounded and cannot be fathomed.[3]

In the light of this kind of profound significance, it is perhaps easier to see that the reluctance to change the tradition in any particular has some appropriateness. It is important to make sure that the proposed change does not alter the central mystery which lies behind any particular manner of celebrating it.

I think that it was concern for this mysterious aspect of the problem which was responsible for my initial dissatisfaction with the arguments I had heard for the ordination of women, since they hinged essentially on feminist ideology in general or on the socio-cultural and intellectual aspects of religion. I now realize that the appeal to tradition is powerful for the reasons I have just outlined, but the low level at which that appeal is usually made by those opposing the ordination of women can only be rejected.[4] It is not, after all, the outer forms which must be preserved, but the inner meaning of them. The statement "It has always been done this way" clearly refers only to the outward and visible signs, and not *necessarily* to inward and spiritual graces. And precisely here, I think, it is important to remember that which was stated at the outset: The consciousness of humankind is evolving, and this evolution must inevitably affect our religious observances. While it is certainly praiseworthy to defend the faith, it is surely sinful to fossilize it.

By now it should be clear that the burden of proof rests with those who wish to change a tradition, and they must not only have patience with, but must actually respect the Church's attention to her important function of preserving the essence of the mysteries. Women whose interest in ordination is grounded in a mature concern for the significance and success of the total Christian enterprise will realize that their efforts must be exercised for the benefit of humankind, not just womankind. Petulant expressions of feminist outrage and impatience are inappropriate here. Even if we believe that St. Paul's cultural context has been outgrown and therefore reject his specific prescriptions for the conduct of women, we must surely still subscribe to his timeless principle that in the house of God "Everything must be done with propriety and in order."[5]

Now I should like to explain why I have concluded that the time has come to modify the tradition. As will become apparent, I do not believe that the ordination of women to the priesthood will reverse or negate the tradition, but rather that it will amplify and enrich it. I am convinced that our appreciation of our essential religious mysteries will be greatly enhanced, and that beneficial effects will therefore eventually be felt in all aspects of our culture.

In the following discussion, it will not be entirely possible to separate psychological, theological, and cultural factors since the level of archetypal mystery with which we are concerned involves precisely the level at which such factors are not differentiated, but rather are expressed in the imagery and drama of unified ritual.

It is customary in theological studies to consider the liturgy of the Mass in three aspects. The first is memorial, in which the Mass is considered to be a sacramental re-enactment of an historical event. The second is that of the ceremonial banquet. This is the one which has been ably discussed by Hewitt and Hiatt, particularly when they describe the Eucharist as a "sacrament of feeding."[6] It is the third aspect, that of sacrifice, to which I wish to devote my principal attention. It is true that many theologians either discount this aspect altogether, or else dismiss it as being of minor significance. Nevertheless, much of the objection to the ordination of women in the Episcopal community comes from the Anglo-Catholic wing, and for this group the Mass as a sacrifice is of paramount theological importance. Furthermore, I believe it is under this heading that we find the element of archetypal mystery. There is, after all, nothing particularly mysterious about a re-enactment of an historical event or a ceremonial meal. Our culture abounds with secular examples of both. To exclude women from participation in such ceremonies seems quite clearly anachronistic, not in any way consonant with the rest of their position in contemporary society. It is about on a par with not giving them equal pay for equal work. I think some sociological confirmation of this is to be found in the fact that in those denominations whose theological outlook lays the least stress on ritual mystery, there has been the least opposition to admitting women to full participation in ministry.

Let us therefore consider the mystery. Throughout the centuries there have been written thousands of meditations and theological treatises on the meaning of the specific symbolic use of bread and wine. As we all know, these symbols long antedate the Christian era, and occur in many religions outside the Jewish and Christian traditions. Their full significance is inexhaustibly rich, not only in the psychological but also in the theological mode (these two modes being at least overlapping if not actually congruent). Only a few of these meanings can even be hinted at in a paper of this scope. As nature, the bread and wine represent the typical food of humankind, the fruits of the earth. In addition, they represent the reciprocal relationship humankind enjoys with nature. As Jung expresses it: "Bread . . . represents the physical means of subsistence, and wine the spiritual. The offering up of bread and wine is the offering of both the physical and the spiritual fruits of civilization."[7] But the gifts also represent humanity itself, which includes women as well as men. There are a number of variations of the rites of preparation, and of interest in this connection is the cutting of the priest's wafer in the Russian Orthodox liturgy. Each piece represents a different person or group,

foolish to deny the masculine patriarchal aspect of God as it appears throughout the Old Testament, the feminine aspects are also clearly present even if largely overlooked in traditional theology. For instance, in the beginning of Genesis the "spirit of God" in Hebrew is *ruach*, which is feminine. God's outreach toward his people is nearly always described in feminine terms. An example of this is the use of the feminine Hebrew word *yad* (hand), which is used in the numerous passages where God is said to "stretch out his hand" to his people. It should be remembered that one of the great landmarks in the development of human consciousness was precisely that in which the ancient Hebrew people were enabled to perceive God in monotheistic terms, rather than as a motley collection of gods and goddesses. But in so doing they were not abolishing the feminine aspects of deity in favor of the masculine aspects, but rather they were learning to think of God in a way which could be inclusive of both. In these terms, then, we may say that God is androgynous.

It naturally follows that the Christ is androgynous as well. Of course, for the purpose of the incarnation, so that through the reality of a divine life on earth humankind might be enabled to develop a closer and spiritually more profound relation to God than had heretofore been possible, it was necessary to pick a particular sex in which to incarnate. It seems obvious that given the social and cultural conditions and the general level of human development at the time, there was no choice: For the divine message to be received by imperfect humanity, Jesus in the first century *had* to be and therefore was male, even though the living Christ is androgynous.

In order for us to come to an understanding of the Mass as a ritual which promotes the health and development of human consciousness, it is necessary to elaborate at some length the concept of the androgyny of God as expressed in the *imago dei* which includes both men and women.

I should like to make it clear at this point that I reserve the use of the term "androgynous" to denote a quality of consciousness, and that it does not refer in any way to the biological sex differentiation of male and female. If one wishes to refer to physical sexual expression which is directed toward either men or women, the term _____ to be preferred. This is not a trivial po _____ ings are to some extent andr _____ bisexual. It is only _____ culture with its r _____ practically every _____ confusion betwe _____ cepts has developed.

Now the _____ androgyny of human beings is of param _____ portance, since it would be impossible withou _____ or men and women to enter into one another's consciousness at all. Without it men and women would be hampered in communication with one another to a degree only slightly less than that which humankind encounters in its attempts to communicate, for instance, with dolphins. And it is, of course, for a similar reason that God chose to create humankind "in his image."[10] If he had not done so, we would not have the slightest chance of being able to communicate with him at all. Instead, in his goodness, we find ourselves created in his androgynous image, sexually differentiated at the physical level into male and female, but with at least potential channels of communication built-in between humankind and God.

It is, of course, true that the indivisible relation between body, mind, and soul means that men and women will experience their consciousness differently, and will therefore express it differently in many ways. At this point it is important to remind ourselves that the consciousness of humankind is continuously evolving, and so we may naturally expect that fundamental, enduring principles will be expressed in varying forms at successive periods of human history. There is no question that in the present period are suffering from the ill effects of unfossilized stereotypes about the nature of and femaleness. But attempts to correct these, move forward with the evolving consciousness of humankind, should not tempt us into throwing the baby out with the bath water.

Maleness and femaleness provide a classic example of the general principle of polarity which in itself is a necessary condition for the manifestation of anything in material form, as is evident throughout the known physical universe. We see it, for instance, in the positive electrical charge of the proton and the negative charge of the electron, without which there could be no stable matter at all. It appears as light and dark, acid and base, and in fact it is not possible even to be aware of anything without being aware of something from which it differs, to which at least in some sense it is opposed. Now when we consider this phenomenon in the physical universe, we do not make the mistake of confusing opposition with antagonism. Nor would we think of asserting that a proton is "superior to" or "more spiritual than" an electron. At this level we understand the process: a creative tension between a pair of opposites which unite in a new energy potential—in this case the formation of an atom.[11] Another example would be the elements hydrogen and oxygen, which when united give rise to water. But at the level of human consciousness, where we note the operation of a masculine principle and a feminine principle, both within our individual psyches, and between separate human beings and groups of human beings, our understanding has been woefully inadequate and ineffectual. We have allowed entirely inappropriate categories of superiority and inferiority to contaminate our perceptions and modify our behavior so that we now have before us the sorry spectacle of the opposites, their necessary tension deteriorated into antagonism, chauvinism (both male and female), oppression (again bilateral), and the result is predictable: misery and loneliness for all.

If we examine the history of human culture, it becomes evident that the creative possibilities of the uniting of the opposites of the feminine and masculine principles have never been generally understood or implemented up to now except at the biological level. Here men and women unite, and the third, or child, that arises out of their union shares the nature of both. But at the level of consciousness we have always been in a different situation. Men and women have not united as equal opposites. They have used one another in different ways, so that real union has seldom occurred. Man has imposed his will on woman and has used her for purposes of bolstering up his own insecurities. She has been defined as inferior, as the one who must adapt. Woman has gone along with this because it absolves her of a great deal of responsibility; at the same time, in her heart, she knows better. This is *her* guilt. By encouraging or condoning man's image of himself as superior, his inflation of himself, she has perpetuated his denials of his own finitude. I think this is one reason why men characteristically have much less realistic attitudes about death than women do, tending either to deny it or to be morbidly preoccupied with it. Woman has infantilized man in this sense. She has permitted man to project onto her the role of custodian of the mystery of death. But, of course, this will not work if the role is allowed to become conscious, if the mystery is ever articulated, and so she must keep her dangerous understanding to herself. This undoubtedly contributes to man's perception of woman as destroyer, the moon goddess in her Hecate aspect. In contemporary terms this mythological figure is referred to variously as the overprotective mother, or the castrating woman.

Perhaps at this point I should explain more fully what I mean by the masculine and feminine principles, particularly as these concepts apply to contemporary issues. Unfortunately, this is exceptionally difficult to do in a short presentation without appearing to fall in with the cultural stereotypes. But it may be helpful if I remind you of what I said earlier about androgyny, which is the co-existence of these two principles. First, it is a quality of consciousness; and secondly, all human beings are androgynous. This means that each man and each woman carries within his or her own psyche elements of the masculine and of the feminine principle.

Readers familiar with Jungian terminology will know that it is customary to refer to the contrasexual component of a woman's psyche as her *animus*, and that of a man as his *anima*. These may occur in varying proportions, and may to varying extents be unconscious, and also may be projected out rather than experienced directly. But the potentials are there, within each person, and the task before us is to learn how to use this fact constructively. Let it then be clearly understood that in what follows I am not talking about specific roles or types of behavior, but about qualities of consciousness which have, to be sure, been expressed in ways which are familiar to all, but which we have the power to choose to express differently. Ann Ulanov puts this point exceptionally well when she says that "the way we conceive of and value psychic polarities, which are symbolized most often in masculine-feminine terms, may vary according to historical time and cultural influence, but the fact of psychic polarities and the centrality of the masculine-feminine polarity is a basic structure of the human psyche."[12]

In brief, the masculine principle appears to be characterized by focused awareness, and a primarily task-oriented outlook. We usually equate this with rationality, and without it human culture could never have come into being. The feminine principle appears to be characterized by a diffuse feeling of awareness of the unity of all life and a primarily relationship-oriented outlook.[13] This outlook is not rational, but neither is it irrational, which implies opposition to the rational. A better word would be non-rational, a very rich category whose proper relation to the rational is complementarity. The concept of focused, rational awareness is not to be confused with intelligence, which is an independent variable which is not and never has been sex-linked at any level. Intelligence is a tool which individuals either will or will not be taught and encouraged to use efficiently, depending on the cultural conditions of their upbringing, including sexual stereotyping.

Because of the patriarchal, male-dominated culture which has generally prevailed throughout history, focused awareness has always been highly valued. But since the enlightenment, it has taken a great leap forward, and has been developed to a degree of sophisticated elaboration heretofore unparalleled in history. Women who have wished to take their place in the conduct of the world's affairs have had to acquire their skills in an educational system designed by and for men, and which quite naturally therefore encourages and prizes the development of the masculine principle. The idea that the quality of diffuse, feeling awareness is worthy of equally sophisticated development and elaboration has not been recognized. To be sure, there is much contemporary discussion of the value of feeling and emotion, but most of it seems designed to encourage undifferentiated expression. People too frequently seem to imagine that they must choose between thinking and feeling and as a result one or the other faculty remains largely undeveloped, largely unconscious. In the culture at large, the ideal of rational awareness reigns supreme and unchecked. But we see that this development carries the seeds of its own destruction, as we contemplate its hideous technological fruits.

It is my contention that the last 100 years of struggle for the liberation of women is one important evolutionary attempt to correct this imbalance. It is the beginning of a struggle which I hope will lead to the bringing into function of the feminine principle to the same degree of full conscious development now enjoyed by the masculine principle. I think that for a stable, creative society, it is important that each of these principles be *equally* conscious, and therefore equally available to the ego functions of choice and volition, rather than having the suppressed principle expressed largely through unconscious, instinctual modes of behavior. This equal, harmonious development is much more important than the absolute level of consciousness achieved by either principle. The instability and the evil come from the unbalanced bringing into consciousness of one principle without the simultaneous development of the other.

Let us now return to the symbolism of the Mass and try to see how these reflections illuminate our understanding of it. In particular, let us consider the psychological implications of the idea of sacrifice. What is sacrificed under the forms of bread and wine is nature, humankind, and God, all combined in the unity of the symbolic gift. This only becomes a true sacrifice if the implied intention of receiving something in return is given up. If this is not done, it becomes a magical propitiation rite in the expectation of getting something from God. In order to avoid this, the givers must become sufficiently conscious of their identity with the gift to recognize that they are giving themselves up in giving it. Again I quote from Jung:

For if I know and admit that I am giving myself, foregoing myself, and do not want to be repaid for it, then I have sacrificed my claim and thus a part of myself. Consequently all absolute giving, a giving which is a total loss from the start, is a self-sacrifice.[14]

This idea is particularly important in that sacrificing oneself proves that one possesses oneself, since one can only *give* fully that which belongs to one. The conscious and deliberate character of the gift implies the fullest possible knowledge and control of one's ego. This is why self-examination and confession of sin are such an integral part of the ritual: it is most often the less conscious parts of ourselves which lead us into actions which the more conscious part deplores. So we see that this process is designed to bring into consciousness, and therefore under control, *all* parts of our psyche. This, of course, must include becoming aware of our androgyny. As Ulanov expresses it:

The feminine . . . is a factor which must be recognized as essential for the full exercise of the religious function. Thus, if the feminine is neglected, undervalued, or misconstrued, the result psychologically is a diminishing of one's growth toward wholeness, and the result theologically is that the *imago dei* does not achieve its full stature.[15]

The biological man must become aware of the feminine part of his psyche, his *anima*, and learn to accept and come into harmonious cooperation with her. If instead he refuses to recognize her, she will make trouble for him and lead him into actions which he may well have cause to regret. All too frequently he is likely to handle this problem by projecting his guilt onto biological woman and holding her responsible for his difficulties. Of course an exactly parallel process obtains in the case of biological woman. She must become aware of the masculine part of her psyche, her *animus*, and learn to accept and come into harmonious cooperation with him. Unfortunately, the undervaluation of the feminine in our culture too often causes women to capitulate to this masculine side of themselves, leading them into various behaviors which in the long run cannot help but be destructive both to the proper individuation of their own psyche and to the culture at large. Common forms which this takes include the denigration of men, for since the woman has handed over the reigns of her own being to the *animus* within, what need has she of real men? Or, she may try to go through life in slavish imitation of men and their ways, constantly proving to herself and others that she can "make her way in a man's world." There are many others, all equally pathetic, since all reveal that she has not appreciated her own femininity or recognized that at this crucial juncture in history the whole world is likely to perish if she and her sisters do not learn to develop and nourish their own truest values. To me there is no sadder sight than that of women who betray by their behavior that they secretly believe in the outgrown myth of their inferiority to men. Of course these refusals by members of each sex to become truly whole persons are at the root of the age-old "battle of the sexes."

The imperative task of this generation must be to bring this battle to a close, once and for all.

It is here that the Church has the opportunity to play a decisive role, since the mystery which she celebrates in the Mass represents, as we have seen, the full drama of creative polarity between the masculine and feminine principles in all their forms. The entire ritual symbolizes all that is essential to the fullest development of human consciousness, or, to put it in theological terms, to the process of divinization.

This passage from potentiality to actuality, this transformation to a more highly evolved and creative state can be defined psychologically as the rite of the individuation process. Carl Jung expresses the theologically equivalent language as follows:

> The Mass tries to effect a mystical participation of priest and congregation with Christ so that on the one hand the soul is assimilated to Christ, and on the other hand the Christ figure is recollected in the soul.[16]

To put it still another way, the imperfect human androgyny is reflected in the perfect divine androgyny of Christ. The Church has never been entirely unmindful of the importance of the feminine principle, although in common with the rest of the culture this has generally been expressed in the usual separate and not-even-equal forms. But a careful fresh reading of the Scriptures shows that many of the interpretations developed by the male theologians over the centuries, however illuminating they may have been in many ways, however much they may have contributed to the gradual evolution of our culture, however essential they may have been in laying the groundwork for the steps which now must be taken, have nevertheless distorted or ignored the significance of much that was written about women. Jesus, for instance, was a radical feminist in terms of the culture of his time.[17] The mystics, dedicated as they are to the cultivation of their own souls and their private relation to God, have always come closer to a direct understanding of the questions I have been discussing. The metaphorical language of much mystical writing makes it abundantly clear that the most intense forms of religious experience are actually felt as an ecstatic, liberating union of the masculine and feminine principles. It seems to me that the time has come to make all these intuitions explicit by admitting women to the full range of possible ways of participating in ministry. It is hard to see how our most sacred Christian ritual can effectively mediate the rich symbolism we have found it to contain if we continue to prevent women from celebrating it. To persist in this course I fear is not only socially anachronistic but psychologically and spiritually destructive.

To my mind the struggle for the ordination of women to the priesthood is not only, or even principally, another engagement in the continuing battle for women's rights. No doubt the temptation to pursue it at that level is very great, particularly for those women whose pursuit of their true vocation continues to be ignominiously frustrated. But to fall into that temptation is to secularize the issue, and it is a serious mistake to permit the vanguard of the development of human consciousness to be taken over by the secular arm of society. All secularization partakes to some extent of idolatry, because the secular perspective is never eternal. The Church, by including its women at last in full partnership, should be leading and shaping human development, because only in this way can she effect her role of mediating salvation, to *and through* all humankind.

NOTES

1. *Eternity is not to be confused with everlastingness*, but is rather to be understood as a qualitatively different kind of *time* which is perhaps best expressed by the word *timeless*.

2. The theological developments during the patristic period were essential to the establishment of the western consciousness of historicity. For a thorough discussion of the full implications of this point, see Henri-Charles Puech, "Gnosis and Time," *Man and Time*. (Bollingen Series, New York: Pantheon, 1957), xxx, pp. 38-84.

3. Joseph Kramp, S.J., *The Liturgical Sacrifice of the New Law* (London: B. Herder Book Co., 1926), p. 134.

4. For a good description of the low levels to which the appeal to tradition has frequently sunk, see Emily C. Hewitt and Suzanne R. Hiatt, *Women Priests: Yes or No?* (New York: The Seabury Press, 1973), *passim*.

5. Cor. 14:40.

6. Hewitt and Hiatt, *op. cit.*, p. 41.

7. Jung, C.G., "Transformation Symbolism in the Mass," *The Collected Works of Carl G. Jung*, (New York: Princeton University Press, 1969, xx, Vol. 11) paragraph 384.

8. Kramp, *op. cit.*, p. 55. (quoted by Jung, *op. cit.* paragraph 384.

9. This symbolism has roots deep in the history of

human consciousness. In ancient times a male deity, Bacchus, presided over wine, while the goddess Ceres presided over grain.

10. Harold Bumpus, S.J., "Theological Reflection and Religious Experience in St. Thomas Aquinas," unpublished manuscript. Read by courtesy of the author.

11. For a discussion of this principle as applied to human consciousness, clearly pointing out the dangers of its misapplication, see Jung, *op. cit.* paragraph 438.

12. Ann Belford Ulanov, *The Feminine in Jungian Psychology and in Christian Theology* (Evanston: Northwestern University Press, 1971), p. 146.

13. Irene Claremont de Castillejo, *Knowing Woman: A Feminine Psychology* (New York: G.P. Putnam's Sons, 1973), p. 15.

14. Jung, *op. cit.*, paragraph 390.

15. Ulanov, *op. cit.*, p. 292.

16. Jung, *op. cit.*, paragraph 413.

17. For a succinct exposition on this idea, together with good references to other authors who have developed it, see Alicia Craig Faxon, *Women and Jesus* (Philadelphia: United Church Press, 1973), *passim*.

BIBLIOGRAPHY

Bumpus, Harold, S.J., "Theological Reflection and Religious Experience in St. Thomas Aquinas," unpublished manuscript.

De Castillejo, Irene Claremont, *Knowing Woman: A Feminine Psychology*. New York: G.P. Putnam's Sons, 1973.

Faxon, Alicia Craig, *Women and Jesus*. Philadelphia: United Church Press, 1973.

Hewitt, Emily C., and Hiatt, Suzanne R., *Women Priests: Yes or No?* New York: The Seabury Press, 1973.

Jung, Carl G., "Transformation Symbolism in the Mass," *Psychology and Religion*, (Bollingen Series: *The Collected Works of Carl G. Jung.*) New York: Princeton University Press, 1969.

Kramp, Joseph, S.J., *The Liturgical Sacrifice of the New Law.* London: B. Herder Book Company, 1926.

Puech, Henri-Charles, "Gnosis and Time," *Man and Time.* New York: Pantheon, 1957.

Ulanov, Ann Belford, *The Feminine in Jungian Psychology and in Christian Theology.* Evanston: Northwestern University Press, 1971.

The Jerusalem Bible. London: Darton, Longman & Todd Ltd.; Garden City, N.Y.: Doubleday & Co., Inc., 1966.

Anatomy and Ministry: Shall Women Be Priests?[1]

Emily C. Hewitt

THE debate about opening the priesthood to women has intensified in recent months as the Episcopal Church moves toward a vote on the issue at its triennial convention in Louisville, Kentucky, September 29-October 11, 1973. In 1970, Episcopalians voted by a narrow margin to maintain an all-male priesthood, but decided at the same convention to open the diaconate to women on an equal basis with men. There are many dimensions to the debate: ecumenical, sociological, psychological, practical, theological. This article will review and critique theological objections offered against the ordination of women in the Episcopal Church.

The theological objections to women priests can, I believe, be reduced to two types. The first type draws a circle around the priesthood and gives reasons why the priesthood must be a male role. The second type draws a circle around woman and explains why her "proper" role excludes her from the priesthood. The first type of argument—emphasis on

the importance of a male priesthood—is the more
fashionable one in the Episcopal Church today, perhaps because its proponents are spared the ticklish
task of defining woman's role in all respects.

The First Circle: A Male Priesthood

The most recent book opposing the ordination
of women as priests is the work of Rev. George
Rutler of the Episcopal Diocese of Pennsylvania.
Rutler's objections to women priests do not have to
do with their pastoral or administrative ability. He
goes so far as to say that such tasks are among those
things that "women have often done far better [than
men]."[2] Nor do Rutler's objections have to do with
such practical matters as the family responsibilities
traditionally carried by women.

What Rutler objects to is a woman in the sacramental role, especially a woman in the priestly role
at the celebration of the Eucharist. He says:

Quite simply . . . the priest is an instrument of
God when he consecrates, or creates; the significance of his maleness in this instrumentality is
that it is a symbol of the seminal initiative of
God. The instrument and the symbol become
one: the priest consecrates at the head of the
people because God has singled him out in his
maleness to be Christ for the people, the sum-
mation of the naked man before his mother at
Golgotha and the whitely robed man before the
harlot in the Garden. Sex and Eucharist are
together; the priest with an "identity crisis" will

most usually be the priest who does not understand that his central job is to be a man at the altar.[3]

The importance of an all-male priesthood has been underscored by many other writers. Perhaps the most widely circulated of the recent statements was made by the Rt. Rev. C. Kilmer Myers, Episcopal Bishop of California, in October of 1971. Myers said, in part:

A priest is a "god symbol" whether he likes it or not. In the imagery of both the Old and New Testaments God is represented in masculine imagery. The Father begets the Son. This is essential to the *givingness* of the Christian faith and to tamper with this imagery is to change that Faith into something else.

Of course, this does not mean God is a male. The biblical language is the language of analogy. It is imperfect even as all human imagery of God must be imperfect. Nevertheless, it has meaning. The male image about God pertains to the divine initiative in creation. Initiative is, in itself, a male rather than a female attribute. . . .

The priest acts as the commissioned agent of Christ. His priesthood partakes of Christ's priesthood, which is generative, initiating, giving. The generative function is plainly a masculine kind of imagery, making priesthood a masculine conception.[4]

Another statement which has national circulation included these remarks:

The *essential matter* of the Sacrament of Holy Orders is a *male* human being. Any attempt to change this would mean that, although the words are repeated, an ordination is not effected.

The male has the initiative in creation. The act of blessing, which is the fundamental priestly act, is creative. To say "Bless us" is the . . . prerogative of any minister, but to stretch out a hand and say "Bless this" is to initiate a creation. In this the male priest reflects the creative activity of God the Father. . . .[5]

Another twist was given to the argument by an article published by a priest of the Diocese of New York:

Being a Jew, being a Palestinian, being a first-century man—all these are what we might call, in the language of Aristotelian metaphysics, the "accidents" of Christ's humanity; but his being a man rather than a woman is of the "substance" of his humanity. He could have been a twentieth-century Chinese and been, cultural differences notwithstanding, much the same person he was; but he could not have been a woman without having been a different sort of personality altogether.

It is our belief that the priestly ministry of the

Church (the episcopate and the presbyterate) are indissolubly linked to the person of the incarnate Christ. . . . The priest presides at the altar and says what Christ said, does what Christ did; there is a very profound sense in which, at that moment and in that ministry, he *is* Christ. And Christ was a man.

This fact is reinforced by the additional fact that Jesus chose only men for his Apostles (and they chose only men as their successors).[6]

I find two principal assertions that undergird the claim for an all-male priesthood:

First: That God, acting as God the Creator, is exercising "male" qualities: initiative, generative power, and the like; and that a priest, in the sacramental acts, exercises creative, initiating powers that are distinctly masculine and analogous to God's creative, initiating capabilities.

Second: That the Incarnation in a male human being, Jesus of Nazareth, taken together with the selection by Jesus of a circle of Twelve male followers, sets an unbreakable precedent for the priestly ministry in the Church.

But hearing these statements and accepting them as valid are two different things.

The first assertion rests on the claim that we can identify certain spheres of God's activity as "male," such as initiative and creative and generative power. This claim should immediately be suspect for its anthropomorphism, or more properly, its andromorphism. As Voltaire once put it, "God has made man in his own image and man has retaliated." But we believe that the God revealed in Scripture cannot be contained by anthropomorphic or andromorphic images. Writing in the March, 1973 issue of the *Journal of the American Academy of Religion*, Dr. Phyllis Trible, Professor of Old Testament at Andover Newton Theological School, points out:

> Israel repudiated the idea of sexuality in God. Unlike fertility Gods, Yahweh is neither male nor female, neither he nor she. Consequently, modern assertions that God is masculine, even when they are qualified, are misleading and detrimental, if not altogether inaccurate. Cultural and grammatical limitations (the use of masculine pronouns for God) need not limit theological understanding. As Creator and Lord, Yahweh embraces and transcends both sexes.[7]

In fact the Anglican Articles of Religion provide a warning signal to those who would seek God's male qualities in some designated sphere of his activity. The Articles state, "There is but one living and true God, everlasting, without body, parts, or passions. . . ." Or, as the book of Deuteronomy (6:4) puts it, "The Lord our God is one Lord."

To reject an anthropomorphic conception of God is also to reject assertions about the nature of the priesthood which are based on that conception. If God cannot be said to be "male" in some designated sphere of activity, this rules out the possibility of drawing an analogy between some of God's "masculine" actions and the priestly functions.

Even when its basis in divine analogy is removed, there are still other problems with the statement that the priest shows forth "masculine" attributes such as initiative and creative power. The obvious difficulty is the assumption that such attributes are to be associated exclusively with men. Such a claim does not sit well in a world which knows women as writers, artists, and heads-of-state.

Less obvious, but at least as important, is the assumption that these attributes should be associated with the functions of the priest in the sacramental acts. In the "Agreed Statement on Eucharistic Doctrine," developed by the Anglican-Roman Catholic Commission in 1971, one does not find an emphasis on the role of the priest in the eucharistic celebration. According to that document, the presiding minister's activity seems to be not so much that of initiator or creator, but of vehicle for divine action. It is through the activity of the Holy Spirit that "the bread and wine become the body and blood of Christ. . . , so that in communion we eat the flesh of Christ and drink his blood. The Lord who thus comes to his people in the power of the Holy Spirit is the Lord of Glory."

This should be compared, for example, with Rutler's assertion that "the priest consecrates at the head of the people because God has singled him out in his maleness to be Christ for the people. . ." Not only does the priest not have power on his own to consecrate, the priest is not, finally, Christ for his people. The priest is the one who presides, but Christ is present for the people not in the person of the priest but in the "earthly bread and wine become the heavenly manna and the new wine."

The second assertion supporting an all-male

priesthood rests on the fact that the Incarnation took place in a male person, Jesus of Nazareth, who, with his circle of twelve male disciples, sets an unbreakable precedent for the priestly ministry of the Church. This argument has become perhaps more insistent in the months since the publication of Leonard Swidler's article "Jesus Was A Feminist." Since Jesus does not seem to qualify as a male chauvinist, why did he choose only men for the Twelve?

This argument about the sex of Jesus and the Twelve is deceptive. It appears to take with utmost seriousness the historical circumstances of the Incarnation, but it ignores some very important historical realities, specifically the fact that Jesus' earthly ministry occurred in continuity with God's work for and among the people of Israel. Jesus, Christians believe, was the Messiah anticipated by the Jews. If we see Jesus this way, we will take seriously not only his maleness but also his Jewishness, his Davidic ancestry, and his status as a freeman rather than slave. We will regard all these attributes of Jesus not as accidents, but as having theological significance. Not only did Jesus initiate a new age in the relations between God and his people, he also fulfilled the Law. The Messiah was to be David's royal son: a Jewish freeman. Gentiles held no theological status in Israel, and the position of slaves and women, although it varied somewhat during the history of Israel, was never equal to that of men.[8] None of these could qualify to fulfill the Law.

The appointment of the Twelve should also be understood in the context of Jewish religious thought of the first century. The Twelve are symbolic of the twelve tribes of Israel and serve as the fulfillment of

Old Testament prophecy of the restoration of Israel. Jesus gathered the Twelve in order symbolically to reunite the scattered tribes. And according to Jewish theology, those chosen to represent the twelve tribes would have to be Jewish men.

Urban Holmes, Dean of the School of Theology of the University of the South, has elaborated on the significance of the Twelve this way:

> The fact that Jesus did appoint the Twelve (which is probably a historically accurate record) would have nothing to do with the establishment of an institutional Church as we know it, but would be an eschatological sign in anticipation of the fulfillment of Israel in the Kingdom that was about to come, the Twelve not functioning as apostles (Matt. 19:28; Luke 22:30) but symbolizing the Twelve Tribes of Israel on the Day of the Lord.[9]

The more we take seriously the theological significance of the sex, race, and ancestry of Jesus or the Twelve, the less such attributes look like requirements for Christian priesthood. The personal characteristics of Jesus and the Twelve are significant for the fulfillment of Messianic prophecy made under the old covenant between God and Israel. But they are not therefore determinative for the nature of ministry in the Church, which came into being after the resurrection.

Of course the universal implications of Jesus' death and resurrection were not immediately apparent to his followers. It took time for them to understand that the Gospel was for Gentiles as well as for

Jews. The controversy between those who saw Christianity as a Jewish sect, open only to the circumcised, and those like Paul, who insisted that salvation in Christ was for all people, echoes through the Book of Acts and the Epistles. The early Christians slowly began to realize that in the Church the old theological distinctions between Jew and Gentile, slave and free, male and female, were broken down. Membership in the body of Christ was open to all people, transcending the divisions that had existed under the law. So it is no less a sign of the reconciling work of God that Gentile men can minister in Christ's name than it is for women to do so.

The Second Circle: Woman's Role

We have examined so far the arguments which try to draw a circle around the priesthood as a male role, thereby excluding women. The second type of argument draws a circle around the proper role of woman, thereby ruling out the priesthood. Usually, the circle encloses woman in a subordinate role, but occasionally it is argued that this role is merely "different," not unequal.

Opponents who choose to argue for the subordination of women to men often draw on 1 Corinthians 14:33-35: "As in all the churches of the saints, the women should keep silence in the churches. For they are not permitted to speak, but should be subordinate, as even the law says. If there is anything they desire to know, let them ask their husbands at home. For it is shameful for woman to speak in church."

In this passage, Paul is invoking the story of the

fall to argue that woman should have a subordinate role in church life. According to Genesis 3:16, one of the consequences of the fall was the subordinate place of woman: "Your desire shall be for your husband and he shall rule over you." Yet the same Paul who instructs women to be "subordinate, as even the law says," also asserts that "in the Lord woman is not independent of man, nor man of woman," (1 Corinthians 11:11-12) and in Galatians 3:28, "There is neither Jew nor Greek, there is neither slave nor free, there is neither male nor female; for you are all one in Christ Jesus."

Opponents of women in the priesthood are not, by and large, willing to take seriously the problem posed by these contradictions. They would like to accept *both* the message of Galatians 3:28 *and* the message that women are subordinate "as even the law says." Their way out of this dilemma is sometimes to suggest that the message of Galatians 3:28 does not apply to life in this world, but only to life "at the end of time." They would argue that yes, we are all equal before God, but in this age we are still bound by the conditions that resulted from the fall. One writer dismisses the Galatians passage this way: "(Paul's) remark is clearly intended as eschatological—having to do with 'the last days'—when 'God will be all in all.' In other words, the Galatians passage is irrelevant to the (ordination of women)."[10] The author goes on to challenge those who want the priesthood opened to women to state their criteria for preferring the Galatians passage to 1 Corinthians 14:34 as a guideline for the churches today.[11]

In fact, there are good reasons for preferring Galatians 3:28 ("you are all one in Christ") to 1 Corinthians 14:34 ("be subordinate") as the embodiment of the central message of the Gospel. In the first place, Galatians 3:28 is found in a theological discourse in which Paul is discussing the saving work of Christ; 1 Corinthians 14:34, on the other hand, gives a set of practical directions for maintaining church order. Between the two, we should probably assume that the passage which is basically "theological" in character has more long-term importance and relevance for the Church.[12]

Galatians 3:28 has special theological importance because it is describing the order of things in the kingdom, "in Christ."[13] When we pray the Lord's Prayer, we say, "Our Father, who art in heaven, hallowed be thy name. Thy kingdom come. Thy will be done, on earth as it is in heaven." What we are asking is that God work to establish the order of the kingdom on earth, here and now.[14] We do not ask God to put off his saving work until some "last days" that are always at the other end of the rainbow. We do not know exactly what God's kingdom will be like, but the New Testament gives us some glimpses and one of those glimpses is in Galatians 3:28. We know about the kingdom through our life "in Christ." And "in Christ" there is "neither Jew nor Greek, there is neither slave nor free, there is neither male nor female."

The theological importance of the Galatians passage is underscored by the fact that it speaks of a new order which reverses the effects of the fall.[15] In Romans 5:18 Paul says, "Then as one man's trespass led to condemnation for all men, so one man's act of righteousness leads to acquittal and life for all men." The subordination of women to men was one of the effects of the fall, as we know from Genesis 3:16. In Christ's death and resurrection we are freed from bondage to the sinful conditions of existence that obtained under the fall. If Paul had never written Galatians 3:28, we would be compelled to affirm its principles on the basis of what we know of Christ's work from the rest of the New Testament.

But even if women are equal, the argument continues, God intends women and men to fill separate roles in the life of Christ's Church. The unhappy history of the "separate but equal" doctrine in certain branches of our civil life has been no deterrent to its use in various guises by those who oppose the ordination of women priests. One English scholar remarked: "If women are incapable of receiving Holy Orders, it cannot be just because they are, in the vulgar sense of the word, subordinate to men, but because of the particular way in which masculinity and femininity are involved in the whole dispensation of redemption."[16]

There are, then, different spheres for the ministry of men and women. Woman is urged to follow Christ, but by a particular route. She has distinctive functions in building Christ's kingdom and she should look to Mary, the mother of Jesus, and other prominent Bible women for models for her life. Above all, her role in building the kingdom is associated with her ministry as Christian wife and mother.

According to one opponent of the ordination of women to the priesthood, woman's role flows directly from her biological potential for motherhood:

The femininity of woman is clearly marked out by her bodily functions. By nature she is destined for a different life from the man's. However much she tries to avoid this (and the modern methods of avoiding it are many and full of dangers), she can never really escape it. For every normal woman is a potential mother . . .[17]

By contrast, the same writer states, "every man . . . is a potential priest."[18]

The implications of woman's role as Christian wife and mother have been described in a widely quoted essay by the Rt. Rev. Kenneth E. Kirk, the late Anglican Bishop of Oxford. In his view, "The sex-relation once set up must have priority over all other natural relations."[19] The duties of wife and mother involve the "loving submission"[20] of wife to husband which would be threatened by the ordination of women priests, even if ordained women were celibate. Kirk elaborates on this point:

Even if ordination and matrimony were canonically declared to be mutually incompatible, so that no ordained woman were allowed to marry, and no married women to be ordained, the wife and mother would be severely tempted to arrogate to herself a sexual equality with, if not superiority to, her husband analogous to the position of her ordained unmarried sister; dangerous strains would be introduced into domestic life; and the integrity of the Christian doctrine of the married relationship would be gravely challenged.[21]

The assumptions underlying this view of woman's role should be examined in the light of the Gospel message of the new life men and women share in Christ. The rule of men over their wives is clearly a result of the fall (Genesis 3:16) and is precisely one of those sinful conditions of human existence from which we have been saved by God's work for us in Christ.

Bishop Kirk does have a scriptural basis for his assertion of the centrality of woman's role as mother. He quotes from Genesis 1:28, in which God tells the first human couple, "Be fruitful and multiply, and fill the earth and subdue it."[22] (As this instruction is given by God to both Adam and Eve, one may wonder why fatherhood is not given more emphasis by Bishop Kirk.)

By contrast, we find that Jesus' teaching warns against preoccupation with family relations. In Matthew 10, we read:

> Do not think that I have come to bring peace on earth; I have not come to bring peace, but a sword. For I have come to set a man against his father, and a daughter against her mother, and a daughter-in-law against her mother-in-law; and a man's foes will be those of his own household. He who loves his father or mother more than me is not worthy of me; and he who loves his son or daughter more than me is not worthy of me; and he who does not take his cross and follow me is not worthy of me (Matthew 10:34-38).

Nor does Paul provide support for preoccupation with family relations. In 1 Corinthians 7:7 he writes, "I wish that all were as I myself am. But each has his own special gift from God, one of one kind and one of another." Paul is referring here to his own personal inclination toward celibacy, but he was accepting of married life for those who chose it. Paul emphasizes the importance not of family life, but of the spiritual aspects of the new life we have in Christ, urging Christians to "earnestly desire the spiritual gifts" (1 Corinthians 14:1).

"Earnestly desire the spiritual gifts." Are women who seek ordination to the priesthood mistaken to take this piece of Paul's advice?

NOTES

1. Sections of this essay are adapted from *Women Priests: Yes or No?* (New York: The Seabury Press, 1973), Copyright 1973 by Emily C. Hewitt and Suzanne R. Hiatt, and are used with permission.

2. George William Rutler, *Priests and Priestesses* (Ambler, Pa.: Trinity Press, 1973), p. 62.

3. Rutler, pp. 83-84.

4. C. Kilmer Myers, "Should Women Be Ordained? No," *The Episcopalian*, Vol. 137, No. 2 (February, 1972), p. 8.

5. Albert J. DuBois, "Why I Am Against the Ordination of Women," *The Episcopalian*, Vol. 137, No. 7 (July, 1972), p. 22.

6. John Paul Boyer, "Some Thoughts on the Ordination of Women," *Avé: A Monthly Bulletin of the Church of St. Mary the Virgin*, New York City, Vol. XLI, No. 5 (May, 1972), pp. 74-75.

7. Phyllis Trible, "Depatriarchalizing in Biblical In-

terpretation," *Journal of the American Academy of Religion*, Vol. XLI, No. 1 (March, 1973), p. 34.

8. Leonard Hodgson, "Theological Objections to the Ordination of Women," *The Expository Times*, Vol. LXXVII, No. 7 (April, 1966), p. 211.

9. Urban T. Holmes, III, *The Future Shape of Ministry: A Theological Projection* (New York: The Seabury Press, 1971), p. 12.

10. Boyer, p. 73.

11. *Ibid.*

12. C.W. Atkinson, *A Position Paper in Favor of the Ordination of Women to the Priesthood in the Episcopal Church* (New York: n.d.), pp. 1-2; Krister Stendahl, *The Bible and the Role of Women: A Case Study in Hermeneutics*, trans. Emilie T. Sander (Philadelphia: Fortress Press, 1966), p. 32.

13. Atkinson, p. 2; Stendahl, p. 40.

14. Krister Stendahl, "Women in the Churches: No Special Pleading," *Soundings*, Vol. LIII, No. 4 (Winter, 1970), p. 276.

15. Atkinson, p. 3.

16. E.L. Mascall, *Women and the Priesthood of the Church* (London: The Church Union, Church Literature Association, n.d.), p. 34.

17. F.C. Blomfield, quoted in M.E. Thrall, *The Ordination of Women to the Priesthood: A Study of the Biblical Evidence* (London: SCM Press, 1958), p. 102.

18. F.C. Blomfield, quoted in Mascall, p. 27.

19. Kenneth Escott Kirk, *Beauty and Bands and Other Papers* (Greenwich, Conn.: The Seabury Press, 1957), p. 182.

20. *Ibid.*

21. *Ibid.*, p. 186. For another view see Derrick Sherwin Bailey, *Sexual Relations in Christian Thought* (New York: Harper and Brothers, 1959), pp. 260-303.

22. Kirk, p. 181.

Ministry in the Church

Gregory Baum

IN this century a significant change has taken place in the Catholic understanding of divine revelation. There has been a shift from an extrinsicist to a more immanentist understanding of God's self-communication in history. Instead of regarding revelation as the communication of new truths added to human life from without, theologians have come to look at revelation as the clarification and specification, through the experience of Israel and above all the person of Jesus Christ, of God's redemptive self-communication operative, in a hidden way, in the whole of human history.

Revelation and Ministry

This shift also affects the understanding of ministry in the Church. An extrinsicist understanding of revelation has led to the view that Jesus as the divine founder of the Church created an apostolic ministry

and that his disposition in regard to the subsequent
ecclesiastical government was to remain unchanged
throughout the ages, independent of the culture in
which the Church lives and the needs of the Christian people. Here the act of revelation is regarded as
the communication of divine truth or the granting of
sacramental gifts from a place outside of history,
namely God's eternal abode. Jesus as the divine
founder has provided the Church with an ecclesiastical hierarchy and an organizational pattern that
are to remain valid for all times.

If, however, the revelation in Jesus Christ is not
extrinsic to world history, if in fact it clarifies and
specifies the redemptive presence of God in the lives
of men, then the ministry in the early Church, created by Jesus and the apostolic community, reveals
what leadership in the Christian community ought to
be like and hence has normative value for all times.
The ministry of the early Church does not reveal a
definitive organizational pattern to be followed by
the ecclesiastical ministry in later centuries, but it
presents the Church with revealed norms, valid for
all times, by which the organizational patterns of ecclesiastical ministry must be tested in each age.
Among these norms are a Christian understanding
of authority, a Christian ideal of regional pluralism
and apostolic unity, and a Christian conception of
service, fellowship and participation. The apostolic
community provided the Church of the future with
evangelical norms for Christian ministry, and it is in
the fidelity to these norms that the Church's aposto-
licity consists.

The New Testament also presents various styles
of Christian leadership, all of which are obedient to

the common norms. We read that the apostolic activity concerned with spreading the Gospel and protecting its unity was accompanied by various offices, such as teaching, prophesying, baptizing, presiding at worship, and various forms of diaconia (service). In the New Testament period these offices were exercised by different people in the community. What counts in the subsequent ages of the Church is not the *material* fidelity to the structures of the early Church, but the *formal* fidelity to the norms guiding the ministry in the early Church and to the variety of functions exercised in it.

What follows from this is that the Church in every age is free to adapt its religious leadership to the socio-political ideals of the age and to reorganize its ministry to meet the needs of the Christian people—as long as this religious leadership seeks to incarnate the normative values revealed in the teaching of Jesus and the ministry of the apostolic Church.

This shift in the understanding of divine revelation has been accompanied by new *historical* research, undertaken by Catholic scholars, regarding the ministry in the early Church. While Catholics used to defend the view that Jesus appointed twelve apostles and that these in turn ordained bishops to be their successors, Catholic scholars have now come to realize that this schematic presentation of apostolic ministry contains a significant symbolic message, but in no way corresponds to the actual historical events. In the first place the New Testament speaks of disciples Jesus sent out to preach, which were not among the chosen twelve (cf. Lk 10:1), and later gives the names of apostles, commissioned to spread the Gospel, which were not among the twelve (cf. Rom 1:1, Gal 1:1, Act 14:4, 14). The churches described for us in the Acts of the Apostles and other books of the New Testament reveal a great diversity of ministry and ministerial offices, from the highly authoritarian government of the Jerusalem Church to the largely communitarian churches founded by St. Paul.

The monarchical episcopate, which has become a distinguishing mark of the later Church, is not original: it is due, rather, to a development, taking place at different speeds in various parts of the Church, which united the diverse offices exercised in the community in a single person, the bishop. The idea that Jesus appointed twelve apostles and these in turn ordained bishops as their successors has symbolic meaning, but it does not describe what actually happened.

Catholic theologians believe that the gradual historical development that led to the monarchical episcopate was tested by the evangelical norms of Christian leadership and accepted by the Christian community as due to the guidance of the Holy Spirit, but they are bound to hold, on the selfsame principle, that this development could continue. The Church is not bound to the governmental structure it has inherited. The Church retains the freedom to adapt its ministry to the socio-political ideals of its age and to modify its organization to serve the needs of the Christian people, as long as it remains faithful to the divinely revealed evangelical norms to which this ministry remains ever subject.

We conclude that the Church's ministry is truly apostolic not because of its material fidelity to an ecclesiastical structure of the past (of the apostolic age, or the post-apostolic period in which the monarchical episcopate developed) but because of the formal fidelity of its institutional leadership to the divinely revealed norms given by Christ and the apostolic witness.

Ministry as Revelation

While this more immanent understanding of divine revelation relativizes the inherited ecclesiastical ministry from one point of view, from another point of view it gives it greater significance and power. For according to the new approach, the Christian Church and its ministry are truly revelatory. Through the Church and its ministry God continues to address the human family. As the Church is to reveal what authentic human community is to be like, so the Church's ministry is to reveal what leadership and authority are to be like in a truly human community. Since the world is damaged by sin and partially subject to the powers of darkness, since the human family is internally divided by conflicting interest groups and worldly authority only too often operates according to a master-slave model, the community of Jesus is to reveal what the true destiny of the human family is and what leadership is like that does not violate human dignity. The Church is to be different from secular society. Jesus said to his disciples, "No longer do I call you servants, . . . but I have called you friends" (John 15:15). He also said: "You know that the rulers of the gentiles lord it over them, and that their great men exercise authority over them. It shall not be so among you: but whoever will be great among you must be your servant" (Mt 20:25-26). The ministry in the Church has, therefore, a revelatory or prophetic function: it reveals the oppressive character of worldly authority and it presents an ideal of leadership that serves the true needs of the people.

In most Catholic theological reflections on ministry in the Church, this revelatory aspect has been neglected. Even Vatican Council II, while reminding us that all authority in the Church is meant to be a service, does not examine whether the present hierarchical ministry in the Church reveals the oppressive character of much of worldly authority and provides models for a more human type of leadership in keeping with the freedom of God's children. Since the present age is deeply troubled by oppressions of various kinds, by authoritarian governments, and by exploitations and injustices committed by legitimate institutions, since, in other words, today more than ever "the rulers of the gentiles lord it over them and their great men exercise authority over them," the revelatory witness of the Church regarding what leadership is meant to be according to the evangelical ideal has become an urgent political necessity. Today more than ever before, the prophetic role of the Church's institutional structure is an essential part of its mission in the world.

This revelatory role of the Church's ministry demands that it respond to the socio-political ideal of the age and adapt itself to the needs of the people. Unfortunately, the inherited viewpoint in the Catholic Church has been that the ecclesiastical ministry is a fixed and unchangeable hierarchy independent of contemporary political ideals and that it is up to the Christian people to adapt themselves to the workings of this hierarchical structure. The primary given is the hierarchy, to which the people must conform their lives. While an extrinsicist understanding of divine revelation was able to defend such an ecclesiological position, contemporary theology has made us more critical and taught us to demand an ecclesiastical ministry that regains its prophetic role.

Hierarchy as Caste

The fixed and immovable view of the hierarchy has led to a situation where the ecclesiastical government in the Catholic Church no longer corresponds to the moral ideal of the age. While in modern society we regard the separation of the legislative, executive and judicial powers as a moral requirement for any government, in the Catholic Church we still have a government where the three powers are united in the same men. The men who make the laws are the ones who execute them, and even the ones who judge whether they have been adequately applied. According to the evolution of the socio-political ideal and according to contemporary moral theology, such a concentration of power must be avoided in a truly moral society.

More than that, the Catholic Church presents itself as an organization ruled by monocratic power, i.e., the entire Church and each unit within the Church are ruled by a single person. On every level, government in the Church is "a one-man show." While Catholic theologians used to defend this as an act of fidelity to the apostolic institution and thus linked it to God's revelation in Jesus Christ as the one ruler of his people, contemporary theology has come to see that such a material understanding of fidelity undermines the prophetic function of the Church's ministry. A ministry that is identified with monocratic power no longer reveals the oppressive character of much worldly authority and no longer projects forms of leadership for present society that offer genuine service to the human community.

Since people today have become aware of the oppression of women through the various cultural and religious traditions of the ages, and since the kingdom proclaimed by Christ promises us deliverance from all the elements of oppression, the Church ought to reveal through its ordained religious leadership that men and women are destined to be equal. The ordination of women to the priesthood would restore a prophetic quality to the Church's ministry, educating people to discern the injustices in present society and presenting them with an ideal for the participation of women in the life of society.

These remarks on the revelatory character of the Church's ministry make us aware how much the ordained ministry has become a caste in the Christian Church. Ordination divides the Christian people into priests and non-priests. Not only does the sacramental hierarchy fail to reveal the ills of worldly power and propose more human forms of leadership, but it has over the ages become a separate body with special powers and privileges, visibly distinct from the people in style of life, clothing and form of address, introducing the master-servant relationship into the Christian Church and preventing the people from participating in the decisions that affect their lives. To the extent that the ordained have become a caste, they give a counter witness to the New Testament ministry in apostolic succession. Instead of bringing to light the oppressive elements in worldly power, an authoritarian caste within the Church legitimates similar caste formations in the rest of society and gives symbolic support to authoritarian forms of government.

How can this clerical caste system be overcome? How can the ecclesiastical government in the Catholic Church be brought into conformity with the evangelical norms, revealed in the New Testament and valid for the ministry of all ages? According to the proposal of many theologians, the ecclesiastical ministry in the Church must (a) become pluralistic and diversified, (b) reach out for a cooperative mode of exercising authority, and (c) develop a fraternal (and sisterly) style. This was indeed the plan of Vatican Council II, at least on paper. It recommended regional diversity and pluriformity of ministry; it proposed a new ideal of team responsibility and collegial action; and it stressed in a new way that the brotherhood created by faith and baptism is intensified rather than interrupted by ordination. But the ideals of Vatican II are far from being realized in the actual life of the Church.

Ministry and Fraternity (Sisterhood)

Contemporary Catholics have become particularly sensitive to the fraternal (and sisterly) dimension of the Christian life. Their religious experience convinces them that God is graciously present in authentic fellowship, so much so that friendship and equality become for them distinguishing marks of the Church. Class, caste, gender and power divide people in society; yet in the Church, Christians look for a brotherhood that transcends these structures of domination. Contemporary Catholics feel uncomfortable when the men who exercise authority in the Church reveal by their self-presentation—their language, their gestures, their style of arriving at decisions, etc.—that they regard themselves as princes or lords in the community and accept the master-servant relationship as a proper mode of human association in the Christian Church. Lords undermine their own authority in the Church. Catholics are ready to listen to a brother (or sister) who has been placed in a position of authority, but they have begun to suspect that the authority exercised by a master in the Church, however legitimately, does not serve the kingdom of God.

Ordination:
A Questionable Goal
for Women

Ann Kelley and Anne Walsh

WOMEN in the movement are always asked, "What is it you want, to be just like men?" There have always been some women who have called their sisters to more than this. American suffragist Frances Dana Gage, speaking in 1851, urged women to look for a "better country" than the "old land of political, social, economic, and religious privilege" they saw around them. This seems to be an applicable vision for the question of the ordination of women. Do women really want to gain participation in the present clerical structure, even to perpetuate it, or do they want to work for a better and more Gospel-like ministry for all?

Priesthood as Caste

Judging from the practice of priesthood as we know it, there must be a better country for religious leadership than the privileged clerical land we know, one more in harmony with Gospel examples and mandates, one more appropriate to the definition of ministry as believing, hoping, loving service. Priesthood is only one aspect of ministry defined in this way, but we have so identified the two terms of priest and minister that women interested in equality in the Church are forced to consider ordination.

Let us look at what has been made of the ministry of the ordained. Ordination gives those ordained power over other people. Martin Luther said it long ago: when people believe that the sacraments are means of grace, that sacraments are necessary for salvation, and that priests are the usual ministers of the sacraments, then they exercise power over people's souls. It gives the ordained what Hans Küng calls a "global superiority" over the rest of women and men.

Ordination is an entry into a power structure that opens the way to privilege. The priest has access to advantages that lie outside the life patterns of most of the community. Their position exempts them from job hazards, financial worries, and personal responsibilities in ways the rest of the world does not share. A priest practices his ministry with an immunity from job competence and evaluation that is unknown to other service personnel. Such security is unavailable to most people. Once ordained, always ordained: regardless of performance, the priest still speaks, celebrates, represents, and makes policies.

With the exultation of these men, the rest of the people of God are diminished. Wisdom, discernment, and leadership opportunities are localized in the few, while the collective wisdom of the community or the insights of individual nonclerical members are neglected or repressed. Critical faculties and responsible judgments of the Christian people are not cultivated, for there are authorities to speak to every question. The few elect speak on behalf of the immature others. In effect, the Christian community is divided; there are priests, and there are "others."

It is difficult to picture Jesus validating his ministry by the credentials we use today. Jesus resisted any such signs of kingship. His Incarnation has equalized all men and women, has affirmed them, and has bound them together to build the Church. There are no "others," no marginal persons, no ruled or governed in the community. All persons are called by baptism to commitment and reconciliation; in the community, life itself ordains us. The call to ministry does not make the Church into an unequal society. The charity of service does not create structures of domination.

The question women need to resolve, then, as they work for equality and full sharing in the Church is this: Is the power and privilege of the ordained an abuse and corruption of the office, or is it inherent in office itself? Is renewal of office possible, or does office automatically create an elite group different from the rest of the people of God? Perhaps only experience with offices used differently and by a diversity of people make a definitive answer available. Certainly some of the glorification of the ordained comes not from the office but from the expectations of the people who themselves are caught in a system that has formed their concepts of priests and Church authority. Their formation led them to see the priest as hero. Some of the disillusionment with clerical authority and behavior is accentuated by the turmoils of particular times when the clerical voice and witness is discredited by circumstances, silence, or irrelevance.

The present caste system victimizes priests as well as the non-ordained. They must attempt to meet the expectations of the system and of the community, while holding on to their personal integrity. Maintaining this balance, while being all things to all men and women, while being heroes, is a most difficult job description.

Women as Ministers

Nevertheless, whether it is office or the use of office, it seems clear that the priest is heir to a line of cultic caste system so potent and so fixed that any significant changes will not come from those in power. If the changes come, it will be from those who were excluded from the caste on principle, from women. It is women who have the opportunity to either validate ministry outside the old concepts of office or to so renew office that it becomes what it was meant to be—service, acceptance of the community and accountability to it, responsive to needs, and open to individuality and diversity.

Indeed, the traditions of women in ministry point to works consistent with these principles of ministry. Their work was usually not defined as ministry, so narrowly have we used the term, but it was ministry. Since the early Church their work was not officed; even those women who have taken religious vows have had none of the prerogatives of office. But they have built rich traditions:

> The ministry of women has been that of service. Women have been willing to go anywhere, undertake any cause, make any sacrifice.

> The ministry of women has been varied, suited both to their individual gifts and charisms, and responsive to particular needs of the human community in a given time and place.

> The ministry of women has been marked by those virtues foolish to men; weakness, poverty, and powerlessness. (Frances Dana Gage, quoted in Eleanor Flexner, *Century of Struggle: The Women's Rights Movement in the United States*, Cambridge, Harvard Univ., 1959.)

We see moving examples of these characteristics in our time. Women like Dorothy Day, Mother Theresa of Calcutta, Edith Stein and countless others have done work not dictated by ordination. Their concern was justice, not status, and they were able to bring new life to many while being part of them.

Since Vatican II women working in pastoral ministries are called ministers, and they have been able to change the expectations of women and of ministry in their colleagues, their communities, and in themselves. They have not been officed, but have depended on the informal commission and acceptance of the people they serve.

Office, then, is not necessary for ministry, but should some women wish to test a formal identification of office, these ministries cannot be lesser, subordinate, or more private than the priestly office, either by practice or by attitude. Women might strive to combine their past traditions with office, that is, work to make their various ministries, such as serving, healing, comforting, and prophesying, commissioned offices equal but complementary to those of the priesthood. Such commissions should be as valid, as public, and as representative as the priestly ministry. These offices should be different from the deaconial office, but not related to it in an hierarchical sense. The priestly ministry would then become one of many ministries; it would be surrounded by many other forms of officed service in the Church. It then would cease to be a caste. Only then will it be open to women.

Perhaps these ministries would lead to a sacramental commission in response to a call of the community, or new modes of ritualization and expression may emerge appropriate to the particular situation. It may be judged better, rather, to respect the many functions of ministry witnessed to in the New Testament. Experience may even prove that office is not desirable at all. Since the future is so uncertain, women need time and experience to define for themselves the direction which their struggle for equality in the Church must take.

The better country for religious life and values will be difficult to reach. Frances Dana Gage reminded her audience that, "There are mountains of established law and custom to overcome; a wilderness of prejudice to be subdued, a powerful foe of selfishness and self-interest to be overthrown." She added, "For the sake of our children's children, we must begin." . . . a worthy call.

If we want to change the Church-clerical caste system, women will have to think of themselves as models for the future, and go beyond what is the most obvious present sign of equality in the Church, that is, ordination as we know it. Models they may find will probably also recall the origins of Christian ministry, and will point to better ways of ministering for both women and men.

welfare, and will prove to be overthrown. She
added, The life of our children's children, we
must train, we must begin, ...

... want to change the child, cherish the
youth, and we will take up ... of happiness is
useful, ... the duty, and to occupy what is the
... we think, present state of equality in the ... home-
... a ... when we see it. Model's life and
find in myself, who do little ... rights of the ...
... and will point to mercy ... of civilization
... for women and men ...

A New Look at Orders: Ministry for the Many

Thomas F. O'Meara, O.P.

TEN years ago Vatican II began issuing documents which would extensively change the life of Catholics and their parishes throughout the world. The first to appear was concerned with liturgy, with congregational participation and with the replacement of Latin. Nevertheless the decrees of the council never became guidelines for the next 40 or 400 years. They have been supplemented, replaced; change has followed change. The message of the council was that change was possible, that diversity and newness were necessary.

We live in the midst of change. We search, some halfheartedly and fearfully, for ways of fashioning a Christian community (the goal of parish and of diocese) which will be faithful to the Gospel and be comforting to our threatened lives. Some of the ideas and practices even of Vatican II lie far in the past, although the momentum is still present in the struggles of the Church. Living after the turbulent 1960s and amid the uncertain 1970s suggests so many things to be done, so many opportunities to be tested, so many agonies to be faced and consoled.

Church-liturgy-parish-priest-sister. Perhaps nowhere have we witnessed more marked yet subtle change than in the area of parish organization and parish staff. Changes in style and life-style, in garb and status are only signs of deeper alterations. Vatican II did not decree all of this change. What has been happening in many parishes and dioceses is *the expansion and diversification of the ministry*. More people, different kinds of people have been brought into the work of the parish: married deacons, religious education coordinators. Where once the diocese had only a few canon lawyers in its chancery, now there are extensive offices for urban affairs, religious education, social action, peace and justice, diocesan planning, renewal and continuing education. The ministry has expanded.

Can the ministry change, expand? Isn't there only the episcopacy and the priesthood instituted by Christ? And why do we refer to this as ministry (a Protestant word) rather than as priesthood?

The "ministry" is the word the early Christians used for their many activities as Christians; it is related to "deacon." The priesthood is one ministry with its limited role and goals; being a bishop or a deacon are other ways of bringing to life the service of the community. What is this service which the community needs and offers to the world? People today like to argue over whether it is liturgy and Christian education (inner-parochial) or social action (extra-parochial, into the world). The ministry must develop both. The Christian community has two sides, neither of which can be neglected: one nourishes the local community through preaching the Word, celebrating the sacraments, educating women and men toward mature faith. But the community has (in fact, is) a missionary call proclaiming the presence and coming of the kingdom of God amidst our world. The ministry, then, has a large task. Yet, ministers need not be alone, for in fact ministry is not simply the task for ordained, celibate men but, first, the part of the life of the entire community challenging each member.

Roles and assignments expand to meet needs. The past decade since Vatican II has helped us see the wider realm of action for the Christian communities we call "parishes." Slowly, we have seen ministry expand and diversify. Dioceses have now ordained 10 to 100 married men as deacons. Being a deacon, like being a priest (or as the new ordination rite says, "presbyter"), is a way of expanding the ministry of the bishop, the leader and coordinator of the diocesan Church. Tens of thousands of sisters who had carried on the great American ministry of total religious education frequently chose to move out of the school system and into newer areas of justice and peace, or adult religious education, or hospital ministry.

Perhaps your parish has a religious educator, with graduate degrees in education and theology, who is a layman, or a full-time director of the liturgies in the parish. All of this is ministry. It is expanding and diversifying.

There never really was only one ministry. The priesthood once gave the impression of a monopoly. The bishop was seen as only a special priest. The

sisters were trained for the ministry, worked in it
selflessly, were visible publicly as ministers—but
were unrecognized by the Church as such.

One or Many Ministries?

Ministry in the New Testament has many characteristics. Three are especially relevant: (1) all
Christian members in a community have by baptism
a ministry; (2) ministry can have a wide diversification, serving others within the community and
through the community serving the world; (3) ministry is public action. The New Testament exegete
Ernst Käsemann writes:

For Paul, unity in the body of Christ does not
mean the sameness of all the members; it means
the solidarity which can endure the strain of the
differences—the different gifts and different
weaknesses of the different members. . . . A
member of the Christian community does not
represent a static order, although most Christians assume that this is the case. He is constantly representing others and is in confrontation with them. Everyone has his own gifts and
his own duty; everyone is irreplaceable in the
service assigned to him and unmistakable in his
particular capacities and weaknesses. That is
why the apostle is always repeating the watch-
word, "Everyone according to the gifts which
God has given him, everyone according to his
calling."

Every baptized believer in the *ecclesia* has a call to ministry, something to do for the kingdom. Baptism is not an initiation into a frozen state of life where prudent virtue is guarded like a candle in a storm. Baptism implies a general discipleship and servanthood. Naturally there are levels of ministry and office. Apostle, presbyter, bishop, deacon bear an intensity of public and professional ministry in the New Testament, but they do not separate themselves into a priestly caste who alone possess ministry, active service.

There can be many ministries. Today we have only one or two publicly recognized ministries, the priesthood, diaconate. The vast majority of Christians are involved in no ministry. The revolution in the parish is most marked by the parish's introduction of Christians beyond clerics into the ministry *and* by its grass-roots creation of new ministries, especially in education. The triad—bishop, priest and deacon—is one way of realizing leadership in the Church, but it does not claim to exhaust ministry. Ministry is free to realize itself in different ways so that it can meet the needs of the times.

Ministry is action. Now the Christian is a servant but a servant characterized by effort rather than by lowly condition or humble waiting. St. Paul writes to the Ephesians a description of Christian community realized in ministries:

And to some, his gift was that they should be apostles; to some prophets; to some, evangelists; to some, pastors and teachers; so that the saints together make a unity in the work of service,

building up the body of Christ. In this way we
are all to come to unity in our faith and in our
knowledge of the Son of God, until we become
the perfect Man, fully mature with the fullness
of Christ himself (4:11-14).

This view of ministry-in-community comes from a
time Christians accept as the fruitful beginning of
the revelation and Church of Jesus Christ. Certainly
Ephesians involves action. A prophet speaks openly
and publicly the presence and future of Jesus Christ;
an evangelist announces for the community good
news; a pastor and a teacher actually do what their
titles state.

The Word of God is heard but also done. John
has the remarkable phrase that we should "do the
truth" (3:21). Previously, action was translated into
the practice, mainly interior, of private virtues. The
New Testament is not content with private religion.
With its anger toward interior self-justification and
external phariseeism, the new covenant insists upon
faith and action being inseparable. Faith involves
public action because our lives are public. Ministry
incarnates faith through private charity into the
sphere of the local community, the communities of
man, the kingdom.

Ministry or Life-style?

The way you live is not the same as what you
do. *Life-style is not identical with ministry.* Now
only Christians who enter into the life-style of celibacy have access to ministry (the permanent diaconate
is a hesitant exception to this forecasting further

changes). In the era of monastic prominence, the Church had compelled even the "clergy-in-the-world," the diocesan priests to enter celibacy. The one ministry was then placed behind a single life-style.

More and more we are going to see a reverse. Instead of life-style controlling ministry, a variety of people with different life-styles will be interested in a variety of ministries. Will the official Church be able to face this situation? Until recently, in the atmosphere of a celibate community, young men were trained to a combination of state of life (and status) and the monoform ministry. Women entering a convent were, similarly, entering a schizophrenic world where structures of contemplative monasticism were ineptly linked to the most strenuous activity. The local community has had no voice, no opportunity to discern talent and charism. This may be reversed. A life-style will be chosen because it serves a ministry, or because it serves the spiritual development of the minister. There will be more give-and-take between the two.

Life-style is something different from ministry. Belonging to a celibate community is a charism, complicated because it has relationships to the individual's spiritual growth, to the health and work of the members of the community, to the world as sign and leaven. Marriage is also a charism. Charism is not the same as ministry. A person interested in ministry is influenced by two separate but related spiritual forces: the call to ecclesial discipleship and the charism of a life-style. The life-style need not always precede and dominate as it has in the past. Ministry channels charisms into concrete service.

The early Christians consciously disassociated

themselves from the Jewish and Greek priesthoods. Why? Because these words were heavy with sacral status; a sacral state emphasized class, control, externals. The Christians created their own words, making everyday verbs into nouns. A bishop is an overseer; a deacon serves other people or waits on tables; an evangelizer announces good things; an interpreter discerns. The English language and Latin theology have over the centuries resacralized these words. Bishops and priests came to represent cultic figures in a special state. With some notable and irritating exceptions they are not often found where the action is.

Ministerial action involves the public sphere. As long as most Christians are merely "the laity," American faith is interiorized and separated from the public sphere. Evangelization about the Gospel and social issues is relegated to private judgment. Should public prophecy, i.e., the announcement of the Gospel, confront some of our penal systems with the dignity of the new man? Christian "doing" must be more than the charitable imitation of middle-class life. Ministry means action within the community and out of the community for others. If this is true, ministry is as central as private Christian commitment, as central as life-style. Private virtue is not the touchstone of faith, nor is one particular life-style, e.g., celibacy, a necessary condition for what is the easy burden of every believer.

What Is Ordination?

There is confusion over the act of ordination. We are grasping that ministry has several forms, but the ceremony of ordination seems reserved to the young man entering the male priesthood. This is not so. What is ordination? It is the public, liturgical action of the community represented by its leaders commissioning a chosen and trained person to carry on a part-time or full-time Christian service. Ordination to the diaconate even now is not the same as ordination to the priesthood, or to the office of bishop. There is an ordination, a communal commissioning, an ordination ceremony for each major form of ministry. Sacraments are important because they make visual our belief and hope in the power of the Spirit being present to us. If sacraments are important then we should enter the liturgical, communal, sacramental sphere whenever we can. The diversity of ministries should lead to community celebrations as ministers are added to the diocesan and parish staffs.

Women in the Ministry? Married Priests?

These questions are already answered. Women are in the ministry, by the thousands, but the hierarchical Church is slow in recognizing them. Married men and women are in the ministries of diaconate, religious education and social action, but the Church recognizes only the male deacons. What is happening is that the ministry is diversifying faster at the American parochial level than the universal Church can easily grasp. So we have a gap—between the real presence of ministers and the public recognition (ordination) of these men and women. For that is what ordination is, not ordination to one particular order, the male, celibate priesthood, but the public, liturgical commissioning by the Church of someone ready and trained to act in a particular ministry. Just as there are many ministries, so there can be several ordinations for diverse ministries (we already know that from the episcopacy and diaconate, both different from the priesthood).

Whether women or married men will be selected by the local and universal Church for the ministry of bishop or parochial coordinator (pastor), this question receives the notoriety, but it is only a limited aspect of the issue. The major issue is clear; the breakthrough is accomplished. The parish and diocesan ministry is no longer limited to priests and bishop, but is being diversified—in order to discover the fullness of Christian life-in-community and to face the awesomeness of life in our world.

Toward the End of the Century

From 1963 to 1973—from Selma to Watergate. It is hard to be an adult in America today where money, meat and gasoline are disappearing. It is even harder to be an adult believer, for as the demands of fidelity to the letter of the Sermon on the Mount increase, the dark clouds surrounding our faith moving through the future lower. We will survive only if we find in our parishes real community, the important communion of people which Jesus intended when he called into existence the "ecclesia." We will be supported and will be able to support others near and far through that community only if we rediscover the universality and diversity of ministry. We are all ministers. In the sense of people who do nothing or know nothing, there can be no "laity." But we are not all the same ministers, not even the pastor or the bishop. The coordinator of the difficult and vast field of religious education—that is one ministry. The liturgy or the voice of social justice—that can be another. The pastor and the deacon —they are also distinct and different. This diversity gives us life, fashions and directs vital community, and thereby helps us all to reach not only the end of the century, but the end of the world where Christ, the counter-image of the Church, awaits.

Celibacy as a
Feminist Issue

Clara Maria Henning

THE Catholic Church describes celibacy as "one
of the purest glories of the Catholic priesthood"
(Pius XI), a "most sacred and most salutary law"
(Benedict XV), "a brilliant jewel," and a "divine
gift" (Pope Paul VI). Most priests themselves find
such descriptions amusing, and they are silly. They
call to mind absurd locker-room phrases by which
men describe their genitals, such as "the family
jewels," and can be considered more spiritual ver-
sions of the same. But it is unwise to regard such
catch-phrases as merely silly or amusing. They are
highly sophisticated political slogans. They are to the
government of the Church what "law and order" is
to the present government of the United States.

Laymen have come to accept blindly the term
"celibacy" and rarely think through as to what it actually implies or how it affects our lives. At most we
conjure up the word "unmarried" as an analogy. A
closer examination of the word's meaning and ef-

fects, however, reveals so many negative aspects to "celibacy," that we can consider its use an employment of Orwellian language! It is Doublespeak. We have been taught to accept an unthreatening term and are spared an emotional confrontation with its actual message. We have further always viewed celibacy as primarily the priests' problem; after all, they have to live it. Celibacy is very much a women's problem. This innocuous term has over the centuries created a multitude of evils, most of which prove to be particularly insulting and generally detrimental to women.

The topic of celibacy is usually very quickly absolved by looking at canon 132/1 which dictates that clerics are not permitted to marry and that they are bound to observe chastity. In non-Orwellian language, that canon establishes that the Church does not want its priests to make love. It speaks of sex, and since the Church does not want its male priests to make love to other priests, we can be secure in the conclusion that the thrust of celibacy involves entirely a concern on the part of the legislators that priests do not engage in love-making with women.

One innocent suggested to me recently that celibacy may just imply a prohibition against sexual intercourse as such. Perhaps, she reflected, the law still allows priests to hug a girl friend, kiss her, even engage in some petting as long as. . . . Perhaps overzealous canon lawyers caught the ball and ran. Unfortunately, the idea of celibacy excludes all of these activities and much more.

The concept of celibacy precludes any close association with women. The law clearly expects that any relationship between priests and women, no matter how innocent, will lead to better things.

The most blatant expressions of the Church's concern about the sex lives of its priests are found in now repealed diocesan statutes which provided that no priest may ride in the front seat of a car with a woman. We can still point to the present canonical restrictions against housekeepers in rectories as living examples: women employed as housekeepers to priests must either be close relatives or otherwise of an age "past suspicion" (canon 133/1). "Past suspicion" is usually interpreted to lie between the ages of 40 and 50. It would be too charitable to laugh this canon off as mere ignorance or a reflection of past attitudes when the prevalent opinion in medicine, psychiatry, and culture in general was that women had no sex drive at all. Canon 133/1 reveals that the Church suspects its priests to be so sex starved that they cannot be expected to resist any woman at all unless she is old or at least middle-aged. Primarily, however, we should recognize the political import of this simple rule: Celibacy is enforced at the expense of women's self-worth and self-image; the law verbalizes that any woman who has not yet reached menopause is under suspicion and strongly implies that she can be expected to seduce any priest.

Economically, also, there is a message in 133/1. That canon prevents any younger, single woman or one with small children from earning a livelihood as housekeeper to priests.

If life were simple and love an uninviting pastime, we might be able to regard celibacy as a charming idiosyncrasy of Catholic culture. But life is complex and love a universal need. Consequently, a simple law like canon 132 which prohibits priests from marrying cannot stand on its own authority; it must be assisted by complementary regulations such as the insulting and suggestive canon 133.

Priests can, of course, seek diversion outside their rectories. But the concept of priestly chastity demands that men under its obligation are not exposed to contrary influences. Thus we have, predictably, on the books a law which forbids priests to attend public shows: the theatre, movies, the opera (!); dances and picnics are especially out (canon 140). When we think about these forms of entertainment, we recognize that all to some degree involve women: Tosca chased around the table by Scarpia as she cries "Help!"; Butterfly and Pinkerton in the throes of their wedding night; Violetta and Alfredo, Mimi and Rudolfo never getting married but living together; Papageno yearning for a Turtletaeubchen of his own. Women and men, passion and illicit love! Picnics indeed would be dull without beer and girls. The theatre usually depicts the everyday interactions between men and women. Old-time vaudeville and the cabaret at their best can be highly suggestive. And what of movies showing Ann-Margret's pelvic gyrations! The legislators were concerned that priests not be exposed to any of it—they might find out what they were missing. The point is that a rule such as canon 140 is determined to keep priests from sitting next to, dancing with, or looking at women. Feminists are not too sympathetic to Ann-Margret, but they must be incensed at the thought that even the attendance at simple public entertainment involving women is considered "unclean" for the priesthood.

Anyone desirous of keeping a group of people

apart from the rest must count on the contingency that members of the group do manage to break out. Prohibitions against inter-sex associations seem to go so much counter to the general thrust of life that over the centuries ways had to be found by which the class of priests could be effectively segregated. The problem is how to easily identify people who are subject to segregation. Short of tattooing people on their foreheads, clothing is the most readily noticeable and acceptable sign of one's station. Thus it is to be expected that we find rules governing the garb of priests.

The collective consciousness of the Church realizes well that a uniform style of clothing for priests is useful as a tool of control and identification. Canon 136/1 calls for decent ecclesiastical dress at all times; it is, in fact, the basis of a considerable body of literature.

A uniform style of dress and color allow lay persons to recognize immediately that they are dealing with a man separated from the mainstream of their own lives. On the one hand, distinctive ecclesiastical dress serves to mark men as a group to whom all lay persons owe by law respect (canon 119); on the other hand, it keeps reminding the priests themselves that they had better behave. Most importantly, it reminds people that they are dealing with sexual abstainers. Young women are discouraged from flirting; mothers will not take the attitude of "Father, do I have a girl for you!" The clerical collar warns: "Do not tempt."

How clearly the language of ecclesiastical dress announces the wearer's untouchability impressed itself upon me during a recent party. Someone mentioned that a priest walking down the street always reminded him that "he doesn't do it." We all laughed hysterically in sudden recognition of a shared experience. (The same is, of course, true of habits worn by nuns.)

Our Church is too astute and too preoccupied with sex to have missed out on the enormous effectiveness which clerical dress has in imposing a separation between priests and women. Although the language of canons and Church documents on this matter may sound superficially innocent, the ulterior motive gradually impresses itself on the reader. For example, on July 28, 1931, a decree of the Sacred Congregation of the Council admonished that:

> Clerics . . . should be distinguished from the laity even by their dress. There are some who wear even in public garments which are thoroughly secular in both form and color. . . . The result naturally is that the due respect of Catholics toward the clerical order is diminished, and the clerics themselves are exposed to the danger not only of doing things which are foreign and unbecoming to the clerical state, but even, which may God forbid, of falling away entirely from their state.

The intention here is not to make everyone look clean and neat, but to control, and to control the laity as much as the priesthood. "Their state" is celibacy, and "falling away entirely from their state" is loaded language which reeks of sex. With a nod of recognition toward the gay community, let us be sure that all sexual allusions are directed toward— that is, rather away from—women.

Our priests throughout the ages were, of course, no dummies. Despite admonitions to the contrary, many have managed to visit places of entertainment without revealing their clerical state. There are some who are incredibly talented teachers of the theatre (for example, Harke of Catholic University of America). But the taboo is on the books. The following excerpt of a letter from the Sacred Congregation of the Council, dated July 1, 1926, reveals the Church's present attitude about priests who slip into swimming trunks and frolic pool-side just as concretely as it did when written:

> The Sacred Congregation has learned that certain priests . . . when for health's sake they take a vacation in the mountains or at the seashore, or go to the springs . . . to take advantage of the baths or the waters there . . . spend [part of the day] in pleasure-seeking, and go to theatres, revues, "movies," and other such shows which are entirely unbecoming to the dignity of the priesthood. Some even lay aside their clerical garb and dress exactly as laymen, in order to enjoy greater freedom and liberty.

What, one may ask, is wrong with greater freedom and liberty? These immature attitudes have the dual intention of controlling the men and preventing them from attempting any contact with females! I know of no similarly loaded admonitions against the attendance of priests at football, hockey, or basketball games. At most the rules urge restraint in voicing sporty enthusiasm.

The collective conscience of the Catholic

Church is fearful that it will lose control over the clergy and their associations with women. The political question to be asked by women in relation to the above juridic attitudes is: "How dare the Church presume that a group of men of apparently suspect morals can sit in judgment over our affairs? If it feels the priesthood must be kept in check, how can priests guide our lives?" Most directly we should ask: "How can any priest presume to understand women at all if he not only never lives closely with women in marriage, but cannot even associate with women in play and activities of relaxation?" It appears that the "brilliant jewel," the "divine gift" is an adornment manufactured at the emotional expense of women's unsolicited and unrewarded cooperation.

If a system demands celibate males, it is obvious that the schools which feed the system must themselves be all-male and instill in their students a "men only" attitude. Seminary law consequently speaks exclusively of boys and young men as making up the student body (see, for example, canons 1353 and 1354/1). Only "legitimate sons" may enter the seminary according to canon 1363/1. The injustice of this type of segregation to legitimate daughters is evident. A Catholic family, which contributes to the diocese, is in fact supporting a system its daughters are not permitted to make use of. Young girls are expected to stifle any talents and ambitions toward the priesthood. And to add insult to injury, it is generally admitted that seminaries openly teach their young students anti-female attitudes.

How can the men and women in the women's rights movement influence and supervise the seminary curriculum and faculty in this regard? There are a few canons which hint at the possibility of cracking the vicious circle at some future time. Canon 1364, for example, specifies that students should receive an education which reflects their culture and would be suitable to the locality in which the students will minister. Life for women in the United States has changed dramatically over the past few years. Is my local seminary keeping up with these changes? Canon 1364 and some of the interpretive rulings could theoretically afford the women's movement a way of making sure that seminaries teach healthy attitudes toward females—if they were not checkmated by other laws such as canon 1359 which stipulates that the boards of governors of seminaries, who are of course the final authority, must be composed only of priests.

A handful of women faculty members can now be found in minor and major seminaries around the country, but curiously, they are for the much greater part nuns. Nuns are clearly considered much less threatening than other women, and repeatedly preferred on those occasions where the establishment Church admits women to teaching or administrative positions. (See Arlene Swidler, *National Catholic Reporter*, July 7, 1972; I have complained of this in *Momentum*, Dec. 1972 and *Catholic Mind*, Nov. 1973, among other places.) Nuns are preferred even in the seminary kitchen. If the students don't do kitchen detail themselves, they have a few nuns (usually way over 40 and foreigners) to do the cooking. Thus, an average mother of small children looking for a domestic job, or an unmarried Ph.D. in philosophy looking for a teaching post, still finds it enormously difficult to find jobs in a seminary. Average women are effectively prevented from not only exercising an influence on our future priests, but also from earning a living commensurate with their training and inclinations. All this to preserve the future sexual orientation of a few young men!

It is obvious that even if a seminary would voluntarily and publicly revise its curriculum to include women's courses and if it retrained its faculty toward presenting ecclesiastical history and theology with an objective view on females, the pedagogic effect of an environment saturated by maleness and a curriculum and educational goal which verbalizes "no women allowed," cannot but ingrain a very much distorted view on females. Even the most enlightened efforts are wasted as long as the overriding pedagogical thrust is to train young men into attitudes of celibacy.

I am here reminded that there are now seminaries which, in response to over-protectiveness, allow their young seminarians to date. This could possibly be a gigantic step forward, but it could also prove to be a brand new way of manipulating women toward unwittingly collaborating in the preservation of celibacy. Dating in this case is combined with the attitude of chastity; a policy of leniency is combined with one of unswerving strictness, the latter being the determining factor in the seminarians' lives. A policy of dating linked to an overriding policy of celibacy seems to encourage young men to enter into friendships with girls after which they must return to the protective ideology of celibacy. Each encounter affords the young man the sweet decision of his abiding commitment of sexual non-activity. The women are left with nothing but possible heartbreak. Young women alone are placed in a position where once again they may, this time emotionally, support celibacy laws. The irony is that Church history offers us a long period during which exactly the same tactics where employed, tactics through which, as a matter of fact, celibacy was introduced into the life of the Church.

Article 35 of *Sacerdotalis Caelibatus*, the major contemporary document on celibacy of 1967, still dares to instruct that the laws of celibacy were voluntarily accepted by the Catholic priesthood and laity of the 12th century. It is true that Church history reveals a continuous sentiment toward an abstentious clergy. Already the Council of Elvira (*ca.* 300 A.D.) sought to impose celibacy upon a married clergy and consequently upon their unsuspecting wives. This imposition of celibacy was effected through stringent, punitive sanctions against noncompliance. Now, we can express sympathy for the clergy family men involved, but let us ask what of the women involved?

As hard as constantly reiterated celibacy laws may have been on priests, the cruelty levied on their wives seems to have taken no end. There were laws which provided that a cleric may not visit his wife except in the presence of reliable witnesses. There were laws which imposed excommunication on those not ready to desert their families. There were laws which threatened physical punishment to priests. Wives could even be sold! Did the women of those first ten centuries who married clerics have an inkling that eventually they would be compromised to support the Church's idea of celibacy by these insidious means? What happened to their millions over the centuries? How could the Church in conscience ordain married men and then force them into a life of chastity? Are our contemporary seminaries following the same tactics by allowing young seminarians to date? Was the Church of old at all concerned to provide sustenance either materially or spiritually for the families of its newly chaste clergy, and is the contemporary Church at all concerned about the feelings of young girls who date seminarians?

How difficult the Church found it to impose celibacy on the priesthood is revealed by the very fact that it spent almost a thousand years impressing the people with its ideas on sexual purity. And, still, during the Gregorian Reformation (11th century) clerics resisted celibacy laws with threats and bodily violence toward their bishops. I hope that their fury was diligently fanned by their wives and girl friends; in memory of them, we should light a few fires of our own.

To return to the twentieth century and men properly ordained. The document *Sacerdotalis Caelibatus* shows a great interest in reintroducing a system of common life for priests (Article 80). This sentiment is an extension of canon 134 of the *Code of Canon Law*, which "favors" the common life. Communal life was in past ages an economically expedient way for priests to be educated and to find companionship in eating and praying together. Today, however, a return to communal living is clearly seen as an alternative way of keeping men under administrative surveillance. Efforts to reintroduce communal living seek to counter a trend in America which sees both diocesan and religious priests moving into pri-

vate apartments, especially those studying or teaching at universities. It is no secret that there has aris-
en a rather high incidence of priests finding girl
friends and adopting what the code calls an "uncl+eri-
cal life" (see *Newsweek*, Dec. 3, 1973).

Although the Church expresses a well-advised
concern to guard priests from loneliness (Article 93),
the intention of recommending the common life is
clearly to safeguard our priest's chastity:

> Priestly chastity is increased, guarded and de-
> fended by a way of life, surroundings and activi-
> ty suited to a minister of God. For this reason
> the close sacramental brotherhood . . . must be
> fostered to the utmost (Article 79).

Is it merely academic to ask whether the intent of
Article 79 is to keep priests away from women or
women away from priests? We should be aware that
a further separation between priests and women will
exacerbate the gulf of understanding between them.
It is even now practically impossible to see a priest
for any detailed discussion involving, perhaps, the
parochial school or the matter of women lectors
when he lives in an average rectory. Women already
have no forum in which to bring priests to account.
How much more difficult our lives will be when
greater numbers of priests begin living together with
the express understanding that they do so in order to
guard their chastity!
A society which requires sexual abstinence of its
functionaries tends to create rules which in themselves do not mention or even imply celibacy, but
which are, nevertheless, attributable to them. Celi-

bate legislators of a thousand years ago never had the opportunity to engage adult women in conversation. In charity, they may be forgiven for many of our woes, but the same leniency cannot be shown to the contemporary leadership.

Women of the twentieth century are still exposed to some now outrageous attitudes held by eighth, ninth, and tenth century male celibates. Many of these are especially prevalent in the procedural rules of court cases. What are we to say about rules which provide for the close examination of a woman's genital orifice, and which instruct doctors as to how exactly to proceed in a digital examination of a woman's hymen? Aside from the humiliation levied upon untold Catholic women who seek to have their marriages annulled on the basis of non-consummation or impotence, what of procedural rules that specify that tribunal officials are obliged to solicit the opinion of a gynecologist, that is, one gynecologist if they are dealing with a male physician, and two extra male physicians to verify the findings if the examining gynecologist was a woman? (A closer discussion of these rules will be found in the upcoming book by Rosemary Ruether, *Images of Women in the Jewish and Christian Traditions*, Simon and Schuster.)

As modern women and men we can approach such rules with the understanding that, after all, every ecclesiastical legislator and every court official has up to date been a celibate male. We may conclude that it is inevitable that there have been fostered interests of highly voyeuristic character among the collective clergy. But what of the millions of women who already have been and the thousands upon thousands of women who still continue to fall victims to this collective legal perversion? What has anyone's hymen got to do with Christ's teaching to love and care for one another?

It may be conjectured as to whether women and their male sympathizers are becoming overly sensitive about laws which affect them. Some may counsel that we should bring more understanding to the issues, to excuse them. That tactic unfortunately does not lead to change and we need changes desperately. An attitude of total forgiveness would also be our luxury: All generations before us had no choice but to cooperate and believe blindly. We have a moral obligation to vindicate the past millions of women who were given no choice, and we have responsibilities toward the future, to see to it that future millions are given a choice.

Presently, there is no reason to suppose that the Church will revise the rule of celibacy. As recently (for the canonist) as 1919 and 1920, Benedict XV declared that the law of celibacy "cannot be permitted to be in any way brought into question," that it "must be retained inviolate in all its purity," and that "the Holy See will never in any way mitigate, much less abolish, this most sacred and most salutary law." Forty years later, the Second Vatican Council reiterated this stance; it has since been affirmed by Pope Paul with the declaration that celibacy "should today continue to be firmly linked to the ecclesiastical ministry," (*Sacerdotalis Caelibatus*, Article 14). The political significance of this uncompromising attitude for women is that as long as the Church insists on a chaste clergy, it can hardly admit women to the priesthood on equal terms with

men. Since celibacy has proven to be such a weak
proposition, the Church will feel it necessary to seg-
regate men and women, and it cannot afford building female seminaries. The Church will continue to
feel obliged to create sterile environments both phy-
sically and attitudinally to keep women away from
priests, which involves communal living, prohibitions
against attendance at movies and dances, and mandatory clerical dress.

The women's movement in the Church may be
persuaded by a quite perverse form of reasoning that
it should be able to demand that, if the Church insists on celibacy, it should exercise better control
over the clergy and create for them environments
where priests are not exposed to temptations and
cannot—however unintentionally—harm women.
Perhaps the Church is indeed a loving mother and
sagacious teacher in setting down limiting rules; if
these were observed, many women would be spared
many heartaches. The problem with this course of
reasoning is that the clergy will continue to make up
our legislators, confessors, and judges, and that the
cycle of breeding ignorance must be stopped at some
point in history.

It may be entirely unnecessary to preach revolution. Modern times are slowly corroding even the
most adamantly backward notions of the Church's
leadership. Especially, notions of safeguarding anyone's chastity by design are continuously being un-
dermined. They were much better suited to a Euro-
pean life-style of hundreds of years ago when
theories about personal freedom and responsibility,
democracy, co-education, and television had not
even been conceived of yet.

It is today practically impossible not to be influenced by general society and thus to various alternatives. Any woman today could easily get rid of a chastity belt by reaching for a can opener. Any TV set invites celibate men to look closely whether the panty hose are really snug or whether the woman alighting from the airplane has in fact forgotten her eighteen-hour girdle. Today, any priest at a university is very likely to become friendly with any number of women, and vice versa. Not every man or every woman can forever resist being interested in the other and submitting to a possible attraction. Neither should anyone be put into the position of having to.

The problem of the matter is obviously celibacy itself, and the question to be asked is: "Why does the Church feel it is so important for a group of men to have no contact with women?"

There are theories which propose economic reasons as the prime motivation, and those which hold that control and manipulation of the men in the priesthood pure and simple are at the heart of the matter. I am rather convinced that the Church's insistence on sexual purity is rooted in the primitive concept of menstruation as defiling, and on an exaggerated notion of a requirement for ritual purity for sacred things and persons. Remnants of this thought process are still discernible today. When *Sacerdotalis Caelibatus* speaks of the chaste clergy, for example, it speaks of celibacy as a staying away from flesh and blood (Article 21). Flesh yes, but *blood*?

We may, therefore, conclude by stating that the seemingly harmless concept of celibacy has coaxed Catholic culture onto a merry-go-round of self-perpetuating evils. "Celibacy" means "stay away from women," and flowery descriptions, such as "a golden law" or "a sweet yoke of Christ" (Pope Paul VI), hide realities which are particularly insulting to women. Simple prohibitions against marriage for the clergy in many insidious ways cause women to be called names and have kept us away from the mainstream of Church life until we are today politically totally disenfranchised.

There are actually people who believe that the Church will welcome women into the priesthood within the next half-century. Does this mean we would have to accept celibacy? If the above observations *vis-à-vis* celibacy laws and the necessity to devise rules in support of them are true, then what rules might be introduced to enforce celibacy for women ministers? The prospects are mind-boggling. Visions *déjà vu* are crashing in upon me: the history of deaconesses, widows and virgins and their systematic suppression until any woman who desired to spend her life in service of God could realize her ambitions only from within the convent.

But there is every reason to anticipate that the Church will be forced to accept a married male clergy long before it will come to accept the idea of women priests. That eventuality would afford us at least a minimum of influence, for then we can close the door at night and, charging at our man with flying colors, we can say: "Listen, Mr. Big Shot. . . . !"